A. FRANK SMITH, JR. LIBRARY CENTER
Southwestern University
Georgetown, Texas 78626

D1276613

ARCHIBALD HIGGINS

EVERYTHING IS RELATIVE

Withdrawn

MAX – DO YOU THINK ONE DAY PEOPLE WILL GO TO THE STARS?

The Adventures of
ARCHIBALD HIGGINS

Everything Is Relative
Run, Robot, Run
Here's Looking at Euclid
Flight of Fancy
Computer Magic
The Black Hole
Big Bang
The Silence Barrier

The Adventures of
ARCHIBALD HIGGINS

EVERYTHING IS RELATIVE

Jean-Pierre Petit

Translated by Ian Stewart

Edited by Wendy Campbell

William Kaufmann, Inc.
Los Altos, California 94022

Originally published as *Tout Est Relatif* © Belin 1981
published by Librairie Classique
Eugène Belin, Paris

Copyright © 1985 by William Kaufmann, Inc.
All rights reserved.
Printed in the United States of America.

Library of Congress Cataloging in Publication Data

Petit, Jean-Pierre.
Everything is relative.

(The Adventures of Archibald Higgins)
Translation of: Tout est relatif.
Summary: The curious Archibald Higgins investigates the theory of relativity.
1. Relativity (Physics)—Juvenile literature.
[1. Relativity (Physics)—Cartoons and comics. 2. Cartoons and comics] I. Campbell, Wendy. II. Title. III. Series: Petit, Jean-Pierre. Aventures d'Anselme Lanturlu. English.
QC173.575.P4713 1985 530.1′1 85-24017
ISBN 0-86576-068-3

500
P445a
v.2

SOPHIE, I SOMETIMES WONDER...
WHAT, SWEETHEART?
... I DUNNO... IF THINGS ARE WHAT THEY SEEM... IF REALITY IS REALLY REAL...
IF MAYBE THERE'S SOMETHING BEHIND EVERYTHING.
TAKE NOTE! ONE UNIVERSE CAN HIDE ANOTHER.
YOU'VE ONLY GOT TO GO AND LOOK!

SOMEBODY'S PLAYING A VIOLIN.
BLIMEY! THAT'S TORN IT! WE'RE IN THE BLINKIN' CATACOMBS OF PHYSICS.
COME ON! THIS IS GOING TO BE ABSOLUTELY FASCINATING!

COSMIC PARK
MISTER ALBERT
PROPRIETOR - FOUNDER
A
IT'S COMING FROM OVER THERE.

FUNNY WAY TO PLAY A VIOLIN.
ALBERT'S MERRY-GO-ROUND THE FASTEST SHOW ON EARTH $1 PER MINUTE
A ONE-MINUTE RIDE, PLEASE!
JA, JA.
OH, WOW! SLOW DOWN, SPEEDY! THIS ISN'T MERRY AT ALL!

TIME'S UP!
HEY - THAT CLOCK OF YOURS SEEMS TO THINK A MINUTE LASTS 59 SECONDS.
NEIN, NEIN, NEIN. VUN MINUTE PRECISELY!
IT'S A CHRONOPERFEKTA. IT MEASURES DER TIME MIT ABSOLUTE PRECISION.
BUT MINE'S A CHRONOPERFEKTA TOO. WEIRD... IT'S A NEW ONE AS WELL. PERHAPS THE UNION WAS NEGOTIATING A NEW CONTRACT THAT WEEK...
OH WELL, IT'S UNDER GUARANTEE.
THERE'S NOTHING WRONG WITH YOUR WATCH, ARCHIE. IT'S IMPOSSIBLE FOR A CHRONOPERFEKTA TO TELL THE WRONG TIME.
THEN IT MUST HAVE BEEN THAT MERRY-GO-ROUND!

MR. ALBERT – IS IT POSSIBLE TO MAKE THE MERRY-GO-ROUND TURN THE OTHER WAY?
JA, NO PROBLEM. IT'S STILL $1 PER MINUTE, THOUGH.
TIME'S UP!
PFFF...
HMMMM...
HEY!

YOU'VE CHEATED ME OUT OF A SECOND AGAIN!
VOT? NUTTING OF DER KIND!
COME OFF IT! TIME IS TIME, AFTER ALL!
YES YOU HAVE!
NO I HAFN'T!
WHAT DO YOU MEAN?
IF YOU DON' KNOW ENOUGH PHYSICS, KEEP OFF DER MERRY-GO-BOUT! STAY HOME!
I LOVE SCIENTIFIC DISCUSSIONS.
COOL IT, ARCHIE. BOTH WATCHES ARE SHOWING THE CORRECT TIME.
THE CORRECT WHAT? WHAT DO YOU MEAN BY TIME, ANYWAY?
HAVE YOU NOTICED HOW THIS BOY HAS A POSITIVE TALENT FOR DUMB QUESTIONS?
A

MEANWHILE, BACK AT THE FAIR . . .

IS DER TIME VAT'S FLOWINK, JA? DER OLD PRINCIPLE OF DER CLEPSYDRA.
AH, OF COURSE. AND THE RATE OF FLOW IS PROPORTIONAL TO THE DIFFERENCE BETWEEN THE PRESSURE IN THE RESERVOIR, AND THE PRESSURE OUTSIDE.
MEIN SUBMARINE IS EQUIPPED MIT DIVING PLANES, SO DAT DER FASTER SHE GOES, DER MORE SHE DIFES.
AN' THAT MEANS THAT TER MEASURE ITS SPEED, ORL YER NEEDS IS A BLINKIN' MANOMETER WOT'LL MEASURE THE H'EXTERMINABLE PRESSURE...
CRIPES, I GOTTIT!
I SAY, IT HAS A MEAN TURN OF SPEED, YOUR MACHINE!
h'OKAY, HUP VE GO! DER MINUTE IS YUST RUN OUT.
HEY, WOT'S GOING ON? WE'RE ON PAGE 25.

BUT FOR THE MOMENT WE MUST LEAVE MAX AND LENNY TO SORT OUT THE CONSEQUENCES OF THEIR UNDERWATER ADVENTURE, AND RETURN TO ARCHIE...
IT'S KINDA WEIRD, WHEN YOU THINK ABOUT IT. IF YOU MOVE IN SPACE, THEN WHATEVER DIRECTION YOU CHOOSE, YOU ALWAYS SEEM TO BE ABLE TO RETRACE YOUR STEPS AND GO THE OPPOSITE WAY.
TIRESIAS CAN ONLY GO AT A SNAIL'S PACE, SO IT'S EASY FOR ME TO OVERTAKE HIM.
WASTE OF BREATH.
OR I CAN STOP, AND LET HIM OVERTAKE ME.
BUT WHEN IT COMES TO MOVING IN TIME, THINGS SEEM TO BE A LITTLE DIFFERENT...

NO WAITING IN THE PRESENT
WELL, I GUESS IT'S FORBIDDEN TO STAY HERE...
...UNDER PENALTY OF NOT BEING ABLE TO START UP AGAIN.
A
PERSON NAME OF TIRESIAS? A REGISTERED PARCEL FOR YOU.
U.S. MAIL
MR. OR MRS.?
MAKES NO DIFFERENCE.
19
HMMMM – IT'S A CALENDAR.
THAT'S RIGHT, ARCHIE. EVERY TIME YOU PULL A PAGE OFF, ANOTHER DAY PASSES.

NO, NO, TIRESIAS: WE CAN'T ALTER THE PASSAGE OF TIME! TO PULL OFF THIS PAGE, YOU HAVE TO WAIT 'TIL TOMORROW.
OH.

SPACE-TIME

SOPHIE - WHAT IS TIME?
IT'S A DIMENSION, LIKE ALL THE OTHERS. CLIMB ON THE SWING AND I'LL EXPLAIN.
WHAT AN EGG-STRAORDINARY DEE-VICE!

FOR INSTANCE, CAN YOU TELL ME WHY TIME FLOWS TOWARD THE FUTURE AND NOT THE PAST?
SMILE, PLEASE!
NOW WHAT?
HAND ME THE SCISSORS, ARCHIE.

SHE REALLY DOES HAVE LOVELY EYES...
EACH FRAME OF THIS FILM IS USED TO RECORD A SINGLE INSTANT OF THE PRESENT. EACH SECOND OF FILM TAKES TWENTY-FOUR FRAMES. IT CONSISTS OF A DISCRETE SERIES OF SEPARATE EVENTS.
NOW I'LL SHOW YOU SOMETHING INTERESTING. PILE UP THIS SERIES OF FRAMES-EVENTS.
YOU GET A SPACE-TIME.
t
y
x
A SPACE-WHAT?
IF I FILL IN FRAMES BETWEEN THE GAPS TO GET AN INFINITE NUMBER OF THEM, THEN I GET A CONTINUOUS SPACE-TIME HAVING THREE DIMENSIONS.
TWO OF SPACE, AND ONE OF TIME.
t
y
0
x

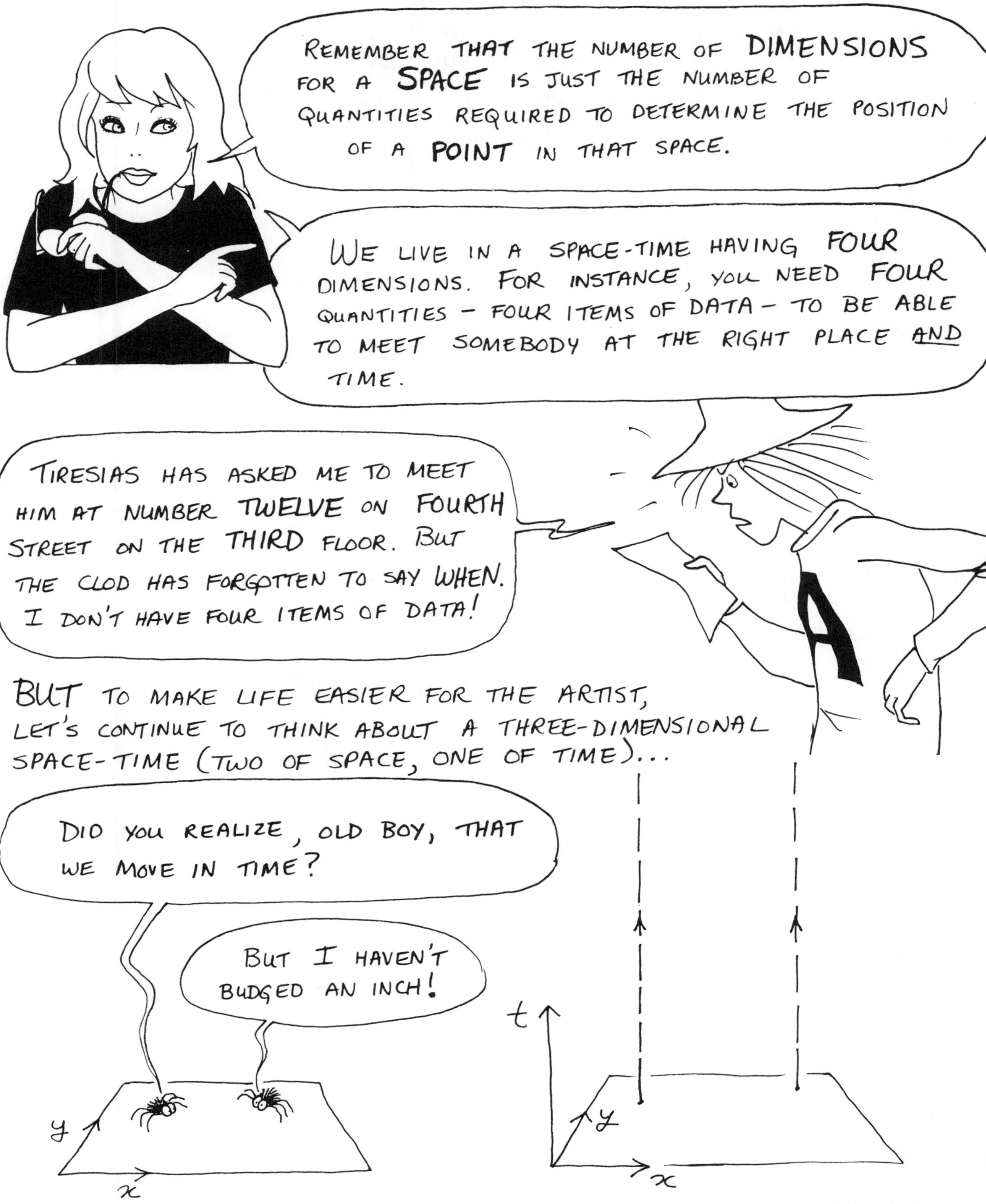
REMEMBER THAT THE NUMBER OF DIMENSIONS FOR A SPACE IS JUST THE NUMBER OF QUANTITIES REQUIRED TO DETERMINE THE POSITION OF A POINT IN THAT SPACE.
WE LIVE IN A SPACE-TIME HAVING FOUR DIMENSIONS. FOR INSTANCE, YOU NEED FOUR QUANTITIES - FOUR ITEMS OF DATA - TO BE ABLE TO MEET SOMEBODY AT THE RIGHT PLACE AND TIME.
TIRESIAS HAS ASKED ME TO MEET HIM AT NUMBER TWELVE ON FOURTH STREET ON THE THIRD FLOOR. BUT THE CLOD HAS FORGOTTEN TO SAY WHEN. I DON'T HAVE FOUR ITEMS OF DATA!
A
BUT TO MAKE LIFE EASIER FOR THE ARTIST, LET'S CONTINUE TO THINK ABOUT A THREE-DIMENSIONAL SPACE-TIME (TWO OF SPACE, ONE OF TIME)...
DID YOU REALIZE, OLD BOY, THAT WE MOVE IN TIME?
BUT I HAVEN'T BUDGED AN INCH!
y
x
t
y
x

THE MOTION OF THESE TWO SPIDERS IN SUCH A SPACE-TIME IS ILLUSTRATED BY THE DIAGRAM ON THE RIGHT.

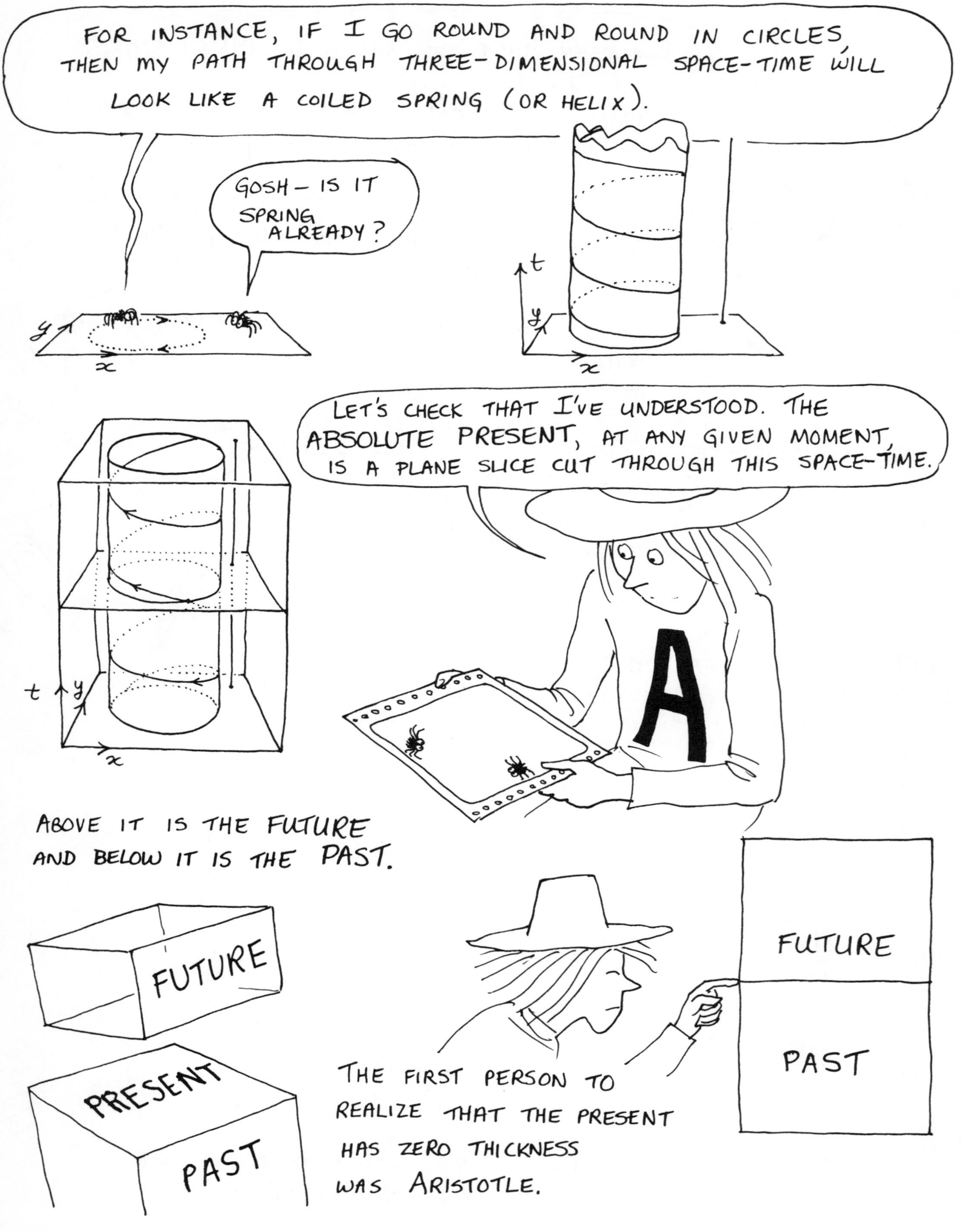
FOR INSTANCE, IF I GO ROUND AND ROUND IN CIRCLES, THEN MY PATH THROUGH THREE-DIMENSIONAL SPACE-TIME WILL LOOK LIKE A COILED SPRING (OR HELIX).
GOSH – IS IT SPRING ALREADY?
y
x
t
y
x
LET'S CHECK THAT I'VE UNDERSTOOD. THE ABSOLUTE PRESENT, AT ANY GIVEN MOMENT, IS A PLANE SLICE CUT THROUGH THIS SPACE-TIME.
t
y
x
A
ABOVE IT IS THE FUTURE AND BELOW IT IS THE PAST.
FUTURE
PRESENT
PAST
THE FIRST PERSON TO REALIZE THAT THE PRESENT HAS ZERO THICKNESS WAS ARISTOTLE.
FUTURE
PAST

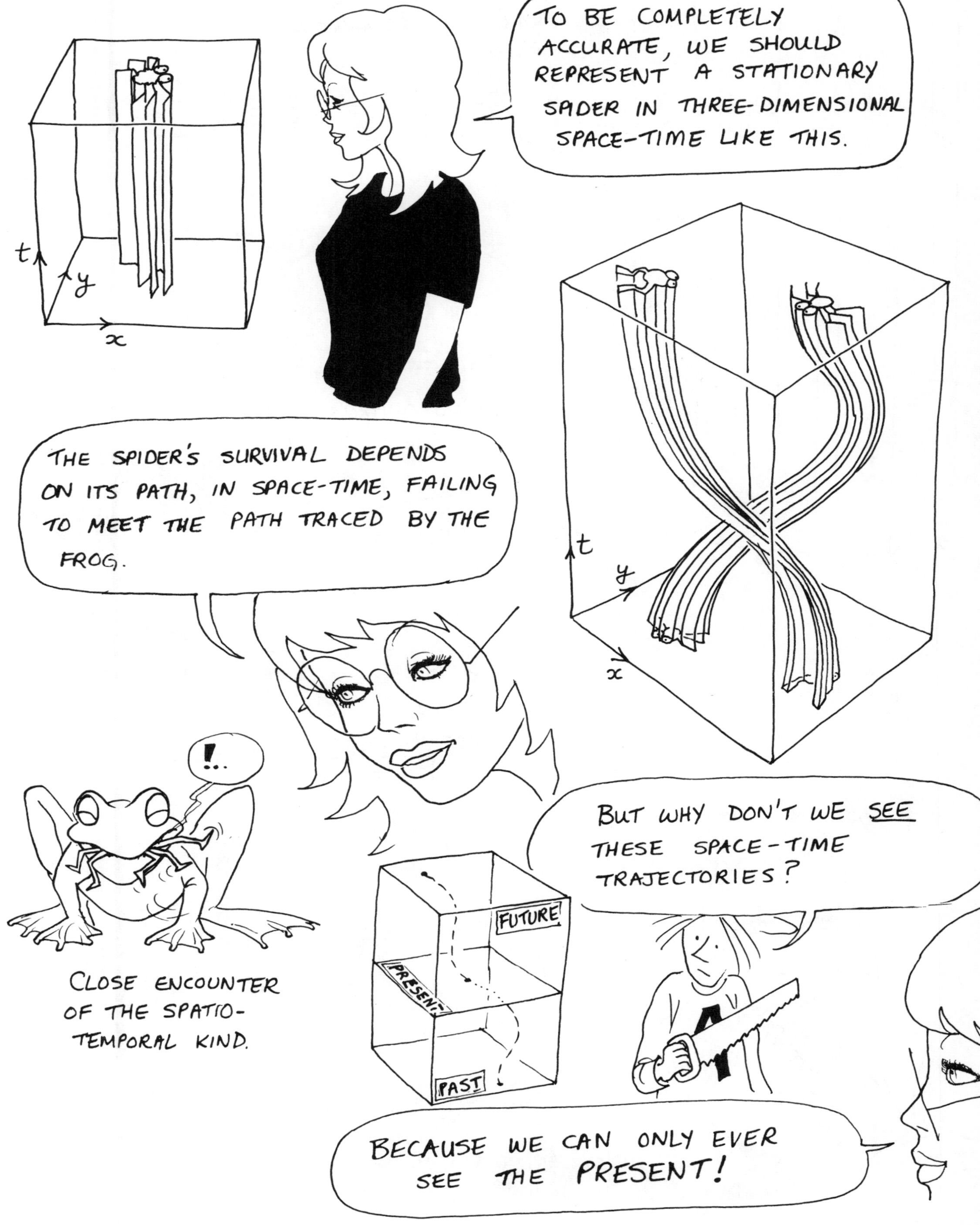

t
y
x
TO BE COMPLETELY ACCURATE, WE SHOULD REPRESENT A STATIONARY SPIDER IN THREE-DIMENSIONAL SPACE-TIME LIKE THIS.
THE SPIDER'S SURVIVAL DEPENDS ON ITS PATH, IN SPACE-TIME, FAILING TO MEET THE PATH TRACED BY THE FROG.
t
y
x
!..
CLOSE ENCOUNTER OF THE SPATIO-TEMPORAL KIND.
FUTURE
PRESENT
PAST
BUT WHY DON'T WE SEE THESE SPACE-TIME TRAJECTORIES?
BECAUSE WE CAN ONLY EVER SEE THE PRESENT!

THE ELEVATOR OF TIME PROPELS US INEXORABLY UPWARD. IT NEITHER STOPS, NOR FALLS BACK.
t
y
x
MON TUES WED THURS FRI SAT SUN
AN ELEVATOR WITH NO DOOR...
... AND NO CONTROLS... HOLY COW!
I'M GLAD SOPHIE'S HERE.
LOOK, SOPHIE — I'VE FOUND A NEW SLANT ON THINGS! I'VE CUT SPACE-TIME OBLIQUELY.
JUST A MOMENT.

THAT'S A TRICK CARTOONISTS OFTEN USE.

y
x

LIGHT CONES

You PROBABLY HAVEN'T NOTICED THIS— but WE ALWAYS SEE AN OBLIQUE CROSS-SECTION OF REALITY.
OH SURE, 'COURSE I HAVE. EH?
ALCOR
MIZAR 1905
1784
ALKAID
ALIOTH 1924
MEGREZ 1905
DUBHE 1865
MERAK 1909
PHEDKA 1901
LIGHT TAKES A DEFINITE AMOUNT OF TIME TO REACH US FROM DISTANT OBJECTS. THE DIAGRAM SHOWS THE TIME AT WHICH LIGHT LEFT THE STARS IN THE BIG DIPPER, SO AS TO ARRIVE NOW.

WALL STREET:
ENTROPY ON THE UP AGAIN
TIME MAGAZINE
FLASH NEWS! SUPERNOVA IN ANDROMEDA!
YOU MEAN THAT NEARBY STARS COULD BLOW UP, AND I WOULDN'T KNOW ABOUT IT FOR YEARS?
NOBODY EVER TELLS ME ANYTHING...
THE IMAGE OF ANDROMEDA THAT WE OBSERVE THROUGH TELESCOPES SHOWS US HOW IT WAS TWO MILLION YEARS AGO.
WE SEE THE SUN THE WAY IT WAS EIGHT MINUTES AGO.
AND MY FEET ARE OLDER THAN MY NOSE!
SO THERE'S REALLY NOTHING HARDER TO SEE THAN THE PRESENT. MAYBE AN OBJECT SITUATED JUST BEHIND MY RETINA...??
NO, ARCHIE. WE CAN ONLY SEE THE PAST. SO AT ANY INSTANT WHAT WE SEE IS THE RELATIVE PRESENT, WHEREAS WHAT WE WERE TALKING ABOUT BEFORE WAS THE ABSOLUTE PRESENT. THE PRESENT IS STRICTLY A PERSONAL THING; YOU CAN'T SHARE IT AROUND.

LET'S TAKE THE DISCUSSION FURTHER. WAVES ON THE SURFACE OF WATER TRAVEL AT A CONSTANT SPEED. HERE A SPIDER HAS FALLEN INTO A POND, EMITTING CONCENTRIC CIRCULAR WAVES.
y
x
IN SPACE-TIME THIS MESSAGE SPREADS OUT ALONG A CONE.
t
y
x
IT'S EXACTLY THE SAME FOR LIGHT, WHICH TRAVELS AT A CONSTANT SPEED OF 300,000 KM/SEC.
IN THE SAME WAY, THE LIGHT SIGNALS RECEIVED BY EACH OBSERVER COME FROM POINTS SITUATED ON A CONE IN SPACE-TIME: THE LIGHT CONE.
t
y
x
IT'S THIS THAT MAKES UP THE OBSERVER'S RELATIVE PRESENT.
YOU MEAN... THE SKY IS A CONE?
YES, ARCHIE; IT'S A THREE-DIMENSIONAL CONICAL CROSS-SECTION OF OUR FOUR-DIMENSIONAL SPACE-TIME.

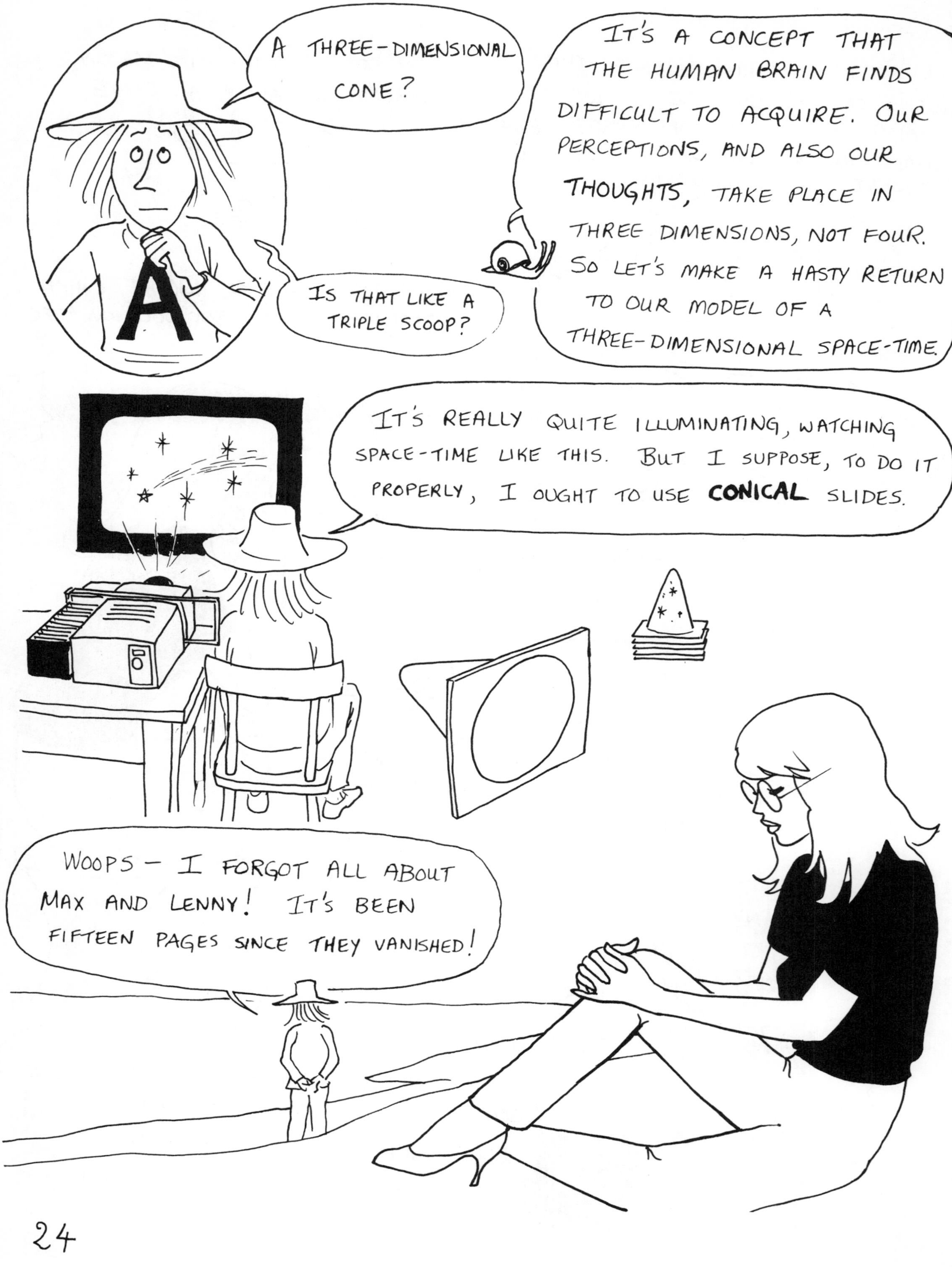
A THREE-DIMENSIONAL CONE?
IS THAT LIKE A TRIPLE SCOOP?
IT'S A CONCEPT THAT THE HUMAN BRAIN FINDS DIFFICULT TO ACQUIRE. OUR PERCEPTIONS, AND ALSO OUR THOUGHTS, TAKE PLACE IN THREE DIMENSIONS, NOT FOUR. SO LET'S MAKE A HASTY RETURN TO OUR MODEL OF A THREE-DIMENSIONAL SPACE-TIME.
IT'S REALLY QUITE ILLUMINATING, WATCHING SPACE-TIME LIKE THIS. BUT I SUPPOSE, TO DO IT PROPERLY, I OUGHT TO USE CONICAL SLIDES.
WOOPS – I FORGOT ALL ABOUT MAX AND LENNY! IT'S BEEN FIFTEEN PAGES SINCE THEY VANISHED!

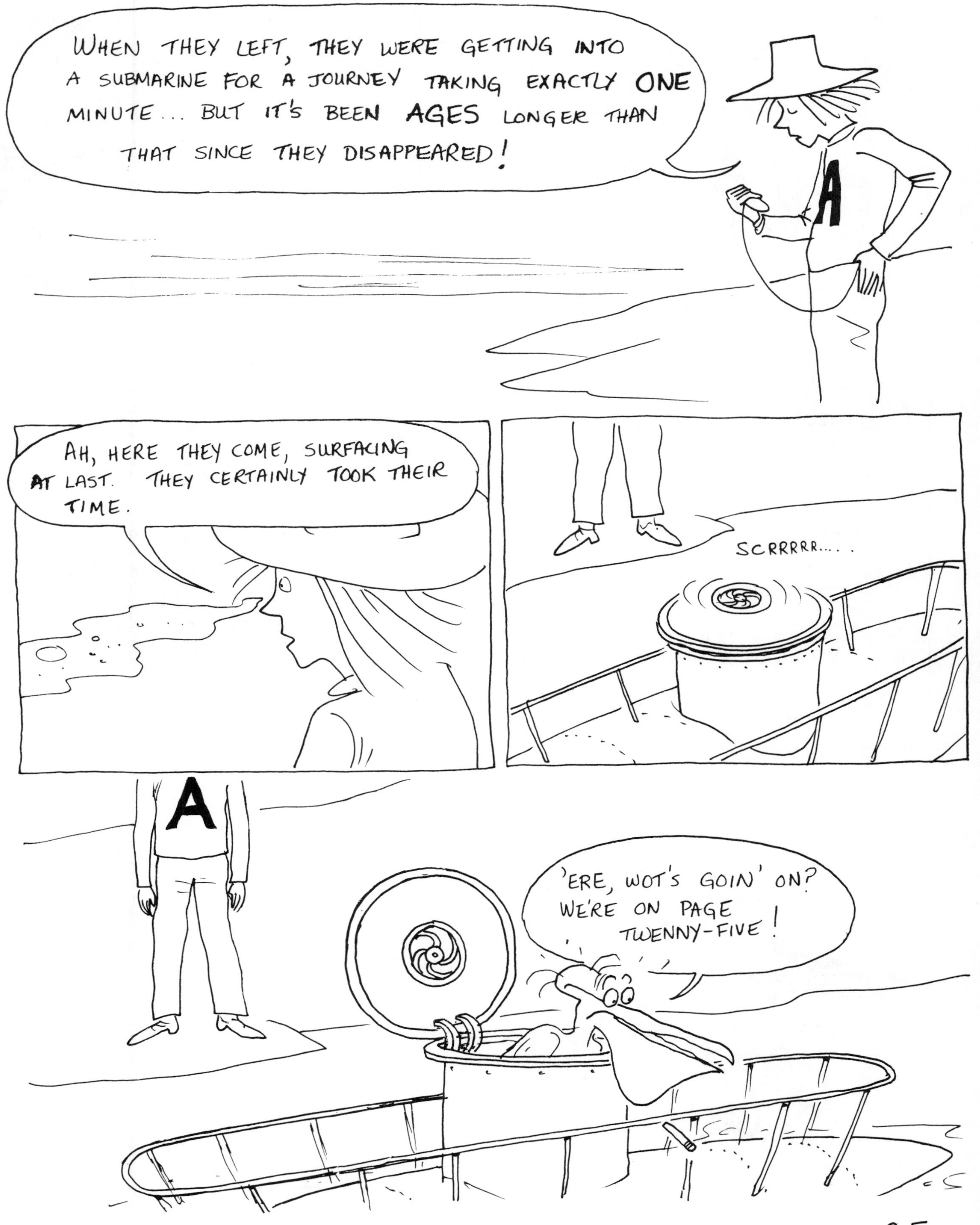
WHEN THEY LEFT, THEY WERE GETTING INTO A SUBMARINE FOR A JOURNEY TAKING EXACTLY ONE MINUTE... BUT IT'S BEEN AGES LONGER THAN THAT SINCE THEY DISAPPEARED!
AH, HERE THEY COME, SURFACING AT LAST. THEY CERTAINLY TOOK THEIR TIME.
SCRRRRR.....
'ERE, WOT'S GOIN' ON? WE'RE ON PAGE TWENNY-FIVE!

JA, JA: VUN MINUTE EXACTLY!
WHAAAAAAT?
IT'S JUST LIKE THE MERRY-GO-ROUND WAS, A WHILE BACK.
TIME, ARCHIE, IS NOT SOMETHING ABSOLUTE.
YER WOT?
DER LADY IS RIGHT, ARCHIBALD— DER FASTER YOU GO, DER LESS YOU AGE.
THEY DO SAY, "TO PART IS TO DIE A LITTLE." BUT THIS SOUNDS MORE LIKE THE OPPOSITE!

NAR LOOK— THAT... CLEPSYDRABLE THINGY WOT MR. ALBERT 'AD... THE 'YDROLLICK WOTSIT... DID IT REELY TELL THE TIME IN THE SUBMARINE?
P_R
OH, JA. LIKE I TOL' YOU, DER CLEPSYDRA IS FED FROM A RESERVOIR AT A CONSTANT PRESSURE P_R. IT FLOWS TO DER OUTSIDE OF DER SUBMARINE, VERE DER PRESSURE IS P_E. SO DER RATE OF FLOW IS PROPORTIONAL TO DER PRESSURE-DIFFERENCE $P_R - P_E$.
DER FASTER DER SUBMARINE GOES, DER DEEPER SHE GOES, AN' DER MORE DER PRESSURE P_E INCREASES. SO DER LESS FLUID DER CLEPSYDRA LOSES. IN OTHER VORDS: DER FASTER YOU GO, DER LESS TIME PASSES.

SOUNDS LIKE A LOAD OF OLD GARBAGE TO ME! HOW WOULD TIME FLOW FOR SOMEONE WHO WAS MOTIONLESS?
MOTIONLESS RELATIVE TO WHAT?
IT'S DER RATE OF FLOW OF A REFERENCE CLEPSYDRA VOT'S PLACED IN A SUBMARINE AT ANCHOR, MOTIONLESS – HENCE ON DER SURFACE.
I'LL SORT THIS OUT ONCE AND FOR ALL!
I WONDER WHAT IT'S LIKE TO BE MOTIONLESS?
2
3
SOPHIE: YOU TAKE NUMBER 2 AND I'LL TAKE NUMBER 1. WE'LL LEAVE NUMBER 3 HERE AT THE MARINA, AND SAIL THE OTHER TWO AT THE SAME VELOCITY $\vec{V}$.
THIS IS ONE DIVE I'M HAPPY TO STAY OUT OF!
1

OH, WOW, LOOK! A CONVOY! THEY'RE GOING AT THE SAME SPEED V, IN THE SAME DIRECTION, AND AT THE SAME DEPTH.
PEOPLES VOT DO EXPERIMENTS ARE PEOPLES VOT'S NOT GOT ANY CONFIDENCE IN DEMSELFS.
MR. ALBERT, SIR: WHAT IS MOTION?
BLEB BLEB BLEB
DAT'S A GOOT QVESTION, TIRESIAS. DER T'ING VOT ACTUALLY EXISTS IS DER RELATIVE SPEED — DER SPEED OF VUN BODY RELATIVE TO ANUDDER. IT'S REALLY QVITE ARBITRARY TO ASSUME, AS VE USUAL DOES, DAT VUN OBJECT — OR GROUP OF OBJECTS (YOU, ME, AND DER MARINA) — IS AT REST. IN FACT, ALL MOTION IS RELATIVE. SO, FOR EXAMPLE... AT DIS MOMENT SOPHIE AND ARCHIBALD, WHO ARE MOVING RELATIVE TO US, ARE MOTIONLESS RELATIVE TO EACH OTHER.

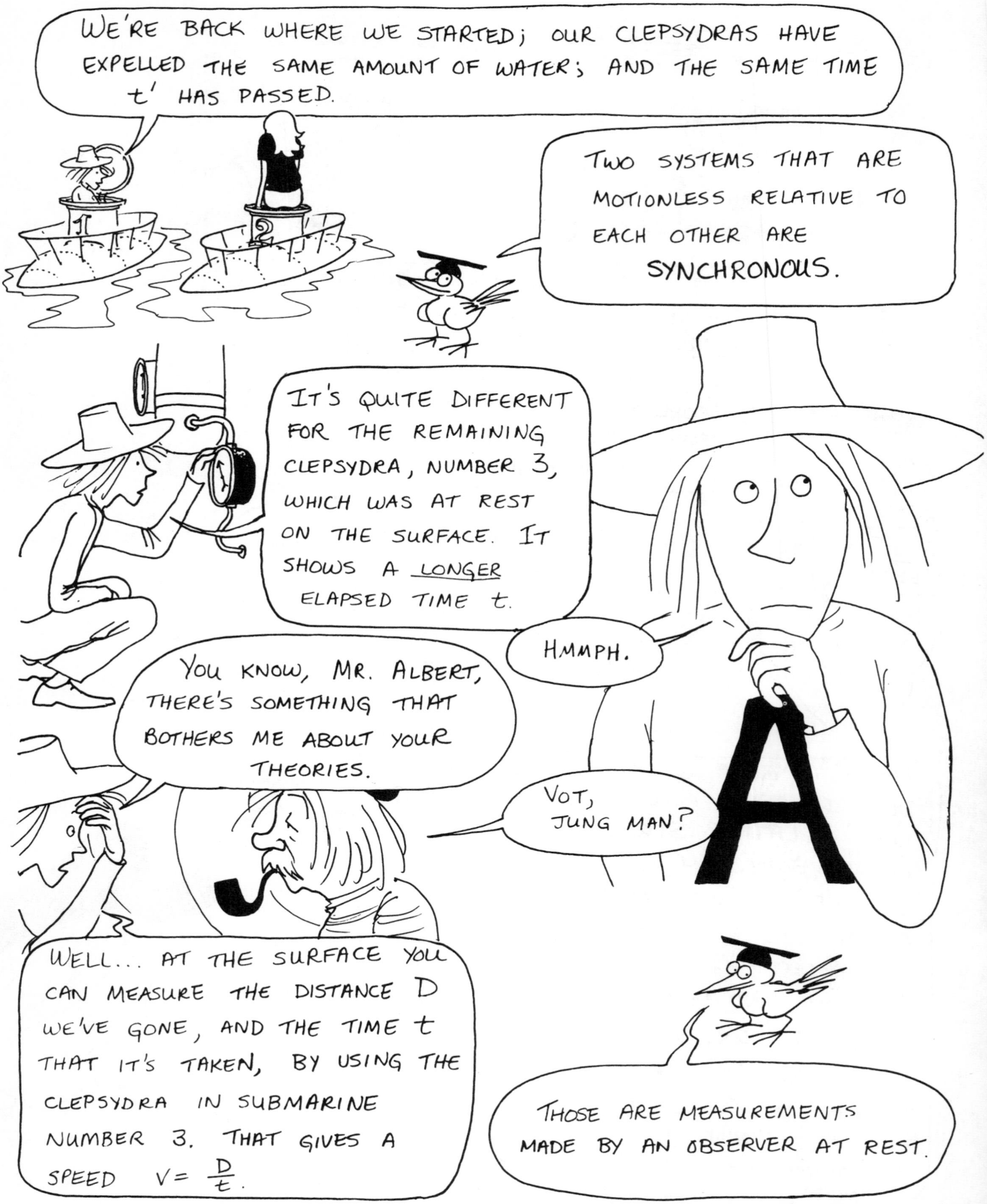
WE'RE BACK WHERE WE STARTED; OUR CLEPSYDRAS HAVE EXPELLED THE SAME AMOUNT OF WATER; AND THE SAME TIME t' HAS PASSED.
TWO SYSTEMS THAT ARE MOTIONLESS RELATIVE TO EACH OTHER ARE SYNCHRONOUS.
IT'S QUITE DIFFERENT FOR THE REMAINING CLEPSYDRA, NUMBER 3, WHICH WAS AT REST ON THE SURFACE. IT SHOWS A LONGER ELAPSED TIME t.
HMMPH.
YOU KNOW, MR. ALBERT, THERE'S SOMETHING THAT BOTHERS ME ABOUT YOUR THEORIES.
VOT, JUNG MAN?
WELL... AT THE SURFACE YOU CAN MEASURE THE DISTANCE D WE'VE GONE, AND THE TIME t THAT IT'S TAKEN, BY USING THE CLEPSYDRA IN SUBMARINE NUMBER 3. THAT GIVES A SPEED V = D/t.
THOSE ARE MEASUREMENTS MADE BY AN OBSERVER AT REST.

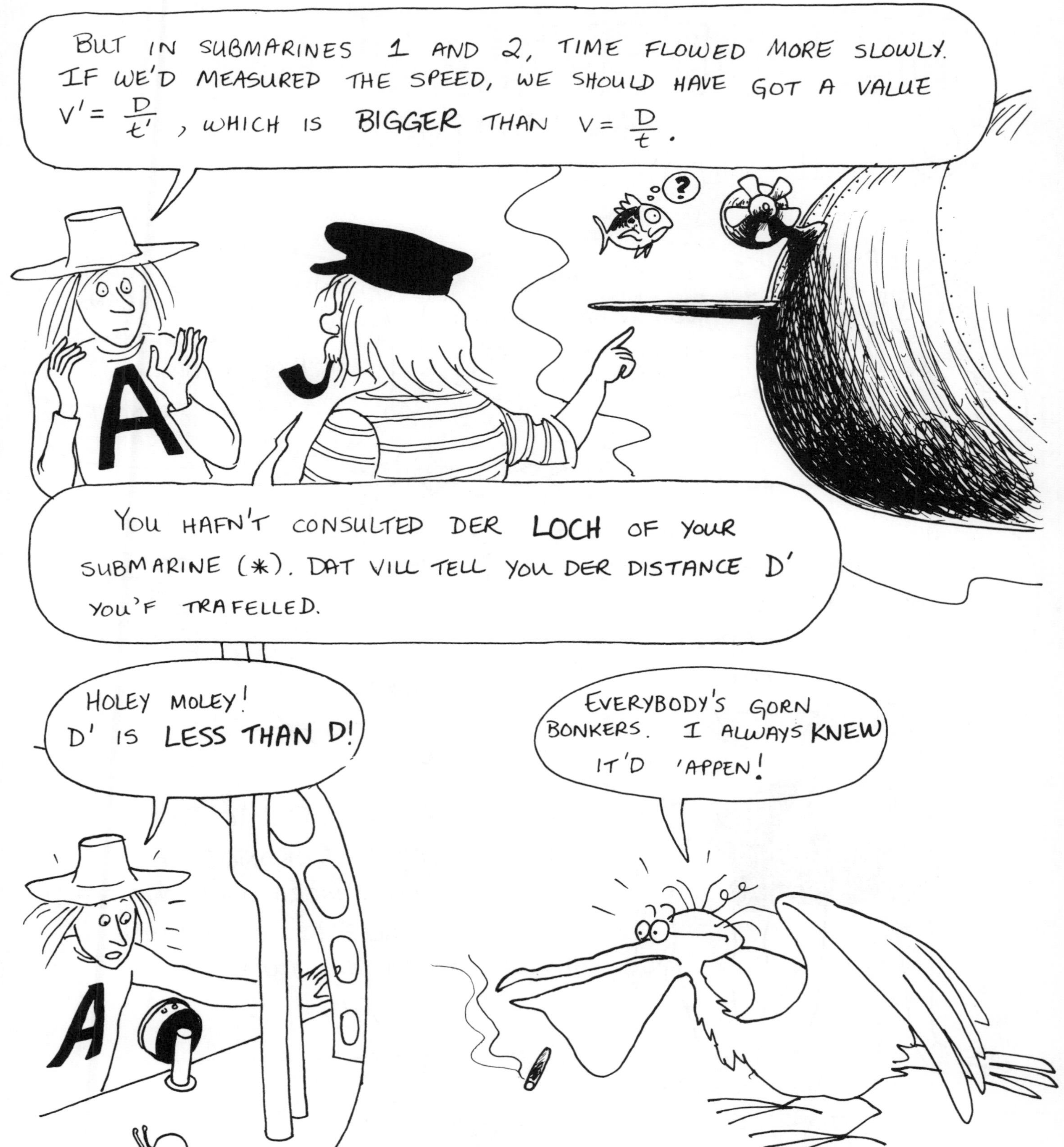
BUT IN SUBMARINES 1 AND 2, TIME FLOWED MORE SLOWLY. IF WE'D MEASURED THE SPEED, WE SHOULD HAVE GOT A VALUE $v' = \frac{D}{t'}$, WHICH IS **BIGGER** THAN $v = \frac{D}{t}$.
?
YOU HAFN'T CONSULTED DER **LOCH** OF YOUR SUBMARINE (*). DAT VILL TELL YOU DER DISTANCE D' YOU'F TRAFELLED.
A
HOLEY MOLEY! D' IS **LESS THAN** D!
EVERYBODY'S GORN BONKERS. I ALWAYS **KNEW** IT'D 'APPEN!
A

(*) THE **LOCH** IS A NAVIGATIONAL INSTRUMENT THAT TELLS YOU THE DISTANCE YOU HAVE TRAVELED.

A. FRANK SMITH, JR. LIBRARY CENTER
Southwestern University
Georgetown, Texas 78626

3 3053 00269 2721

THE LORENTZ CONTRACTION

IT LOOKS LIKE $\frac{D}{t}$ AND $\frac{D'}{t'}$ ARE EQUAL. I GET THE SAME SPEED BOTH WAYS!
BUT... THAT MEANS SPACE GITS SQUORSHED UP LIKE A BLOOMIN' H'ACCORDYON, DUNNIT?
OH 'ECK...
TIMES AND LENGTHS ARE ONLY APPEARANCES. THERE'S NO MORE AN ABSOLUTE TIME THAN THERE IS ABSOLUTE SPACE.
THINK BACK TO COSMIC PARK AND ITS OCEAN, CHRONOS. BUT REMEMBER THOSE WERE ONLY MODELS, DESIGNED TO HELP US UNDERSTAND THE STRANGE STRUCTURE OF SPACE-TIME.

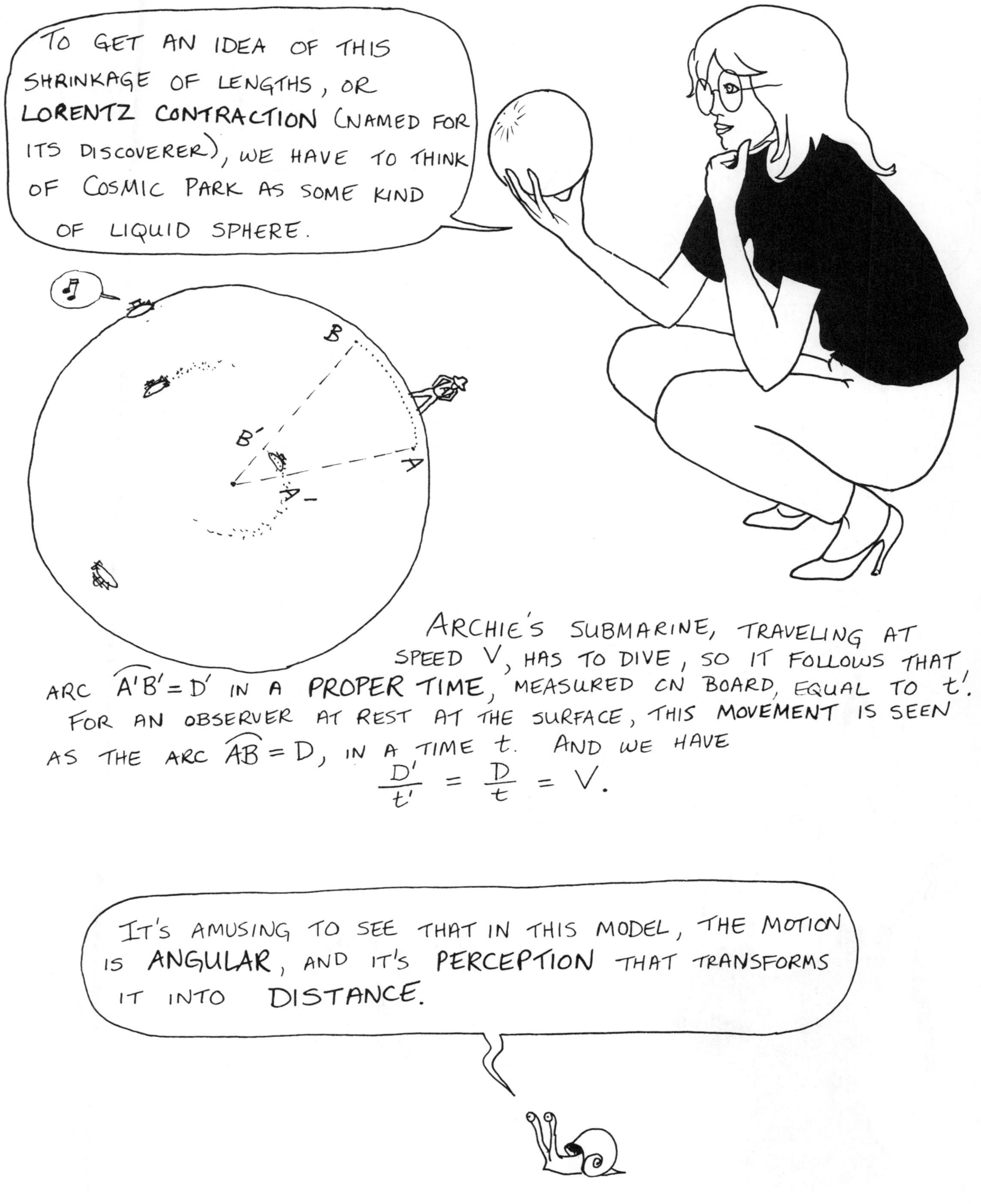
TO GET AN IDEA OF THIS SHRINKAGE OF LENGTHS, OR LORENTZ CONTRACTION (NAMED FOR ITS DISCOVERER), WE HAVE TO THINK OF COSMIC PARK AS SOME KIND OF LIQUID SPHERE.
♪
B
B'
A
A'
ARCHIE'S SUBMARINE, TRAVELING AT SPEED V, HAS TO DIVE, SO IT FOLLOWS THAT ARC $\widehat{A'B'} = D'$ IN A PROPER TIME, MEASURED ON BOARD, EQUAL TO t'. FOR AN OBSERVER AT REST AT THE SURFACE, THIS MOVEMENT IS SEEN AS THE ARC $\widehat{AB} = D$, IN A TIME t. AND WE HAVE
$$\frac{D'}{t'} = \frac{D}{t} = V.$$
IT'S AMUSING TO SEE THAT IN THIS MODEL, THE MOTION IS ANGULAR, AND IT'S PERCEPTION THAT TRANSFORMS IT INTO DISTANCE.

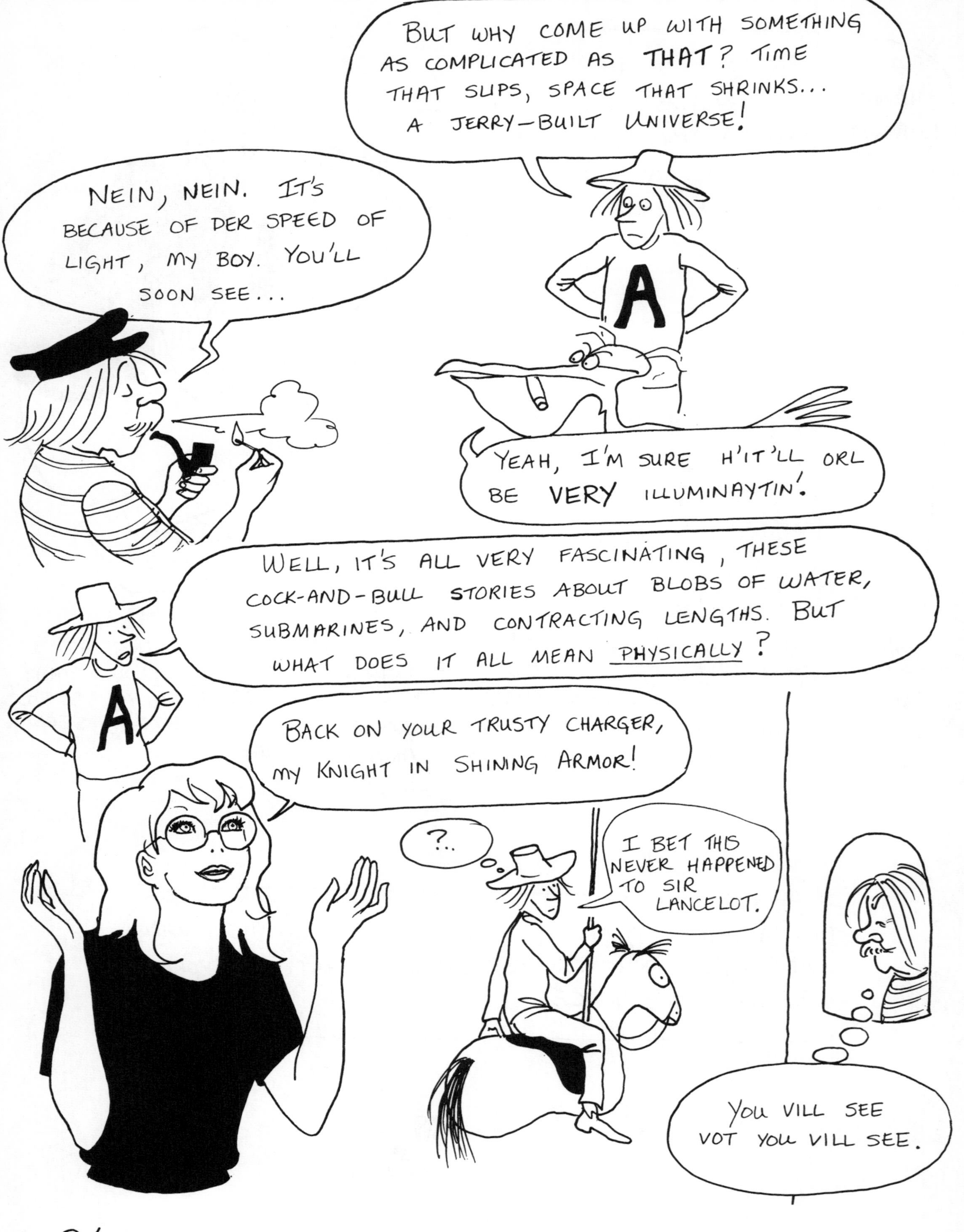
BUT WHY COME UP WITH SOMETHING AS COMPLICATED AS THAT? TIME THAT SLIPS, SPACE THAT SHRINKS... A JERRY-BUILT UNIVERSE!
NEIN, NEIN. IT'S BECAUSE OF DER SPEED OF LIGHT, MY BOY. YOU'LL SOON SEE...
YEAH, I'M SURE H'IT'LL ORL BE VERY ILLUMINAYTIN'.
WELL, IT'S ALL VERY FASCINATING, THESE COCK-AND-BULL STORIES ABOUT BLOBS OF WATER, SUBMARINES, AND CONTRACTING LENGTHS. BUT WHAT DOES IT ALL MEAN PHYSICALLY?
BACK ON YOUR TRUSTY CHARGER, MY KNIGHT IN SHINING ARMOR!
?..
I BET THIS NEVER HAPPENED TO SIR LANCELOT.
YOU VILL SEE VOT YOU VILL SEE.

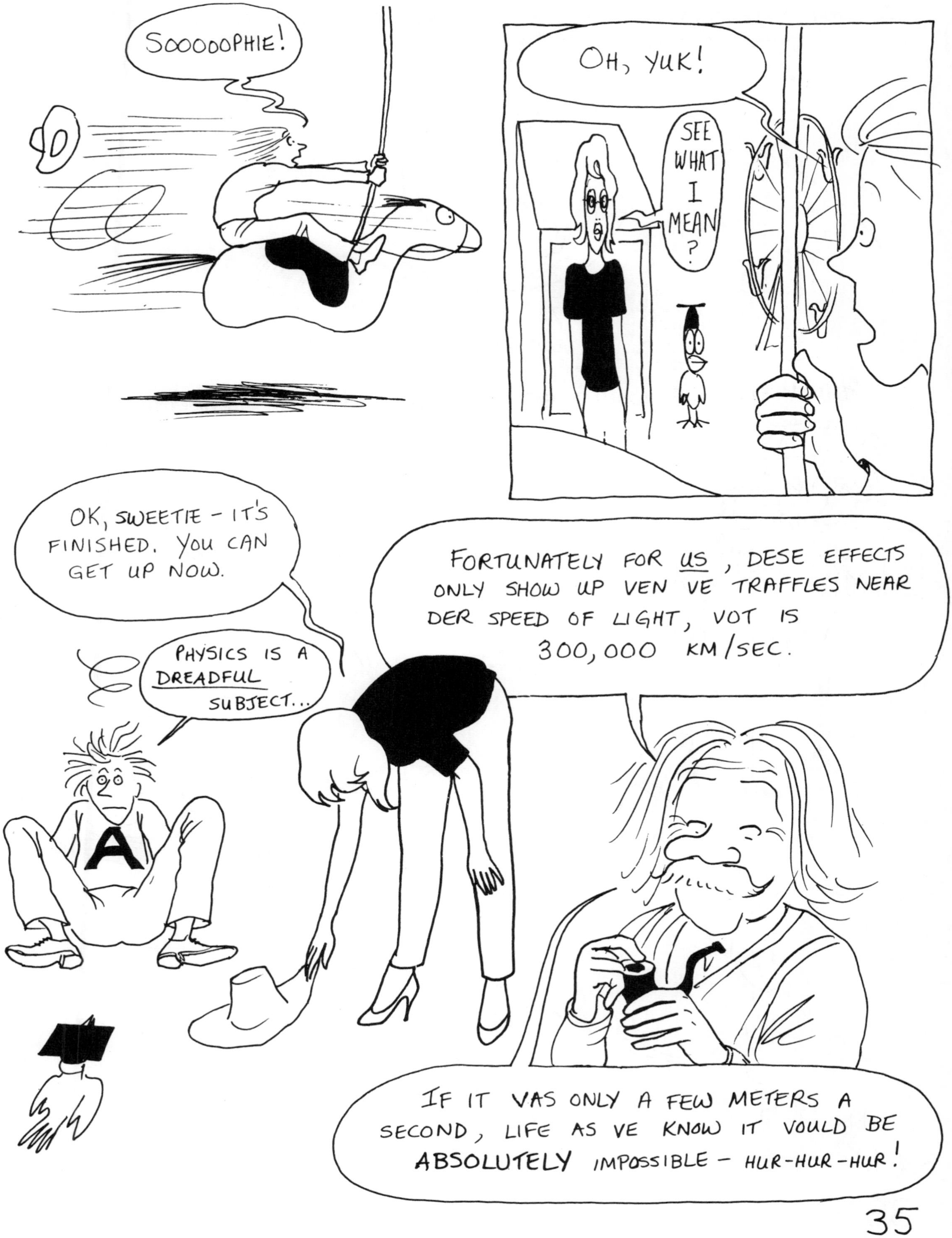
SOOOOOPHIE!
OH, YUK!
SEE WHAT I MEAN?
OK, SWEETIE - IT'S FINISHED. YOU CAN GET UP NOW.
PHYSICS IS A DREADFUL SUBJECT...
FORTUNATELY FOR US, DESE EFFECTS ONLY SHOW UP VEN VE TRAFFLES NEAR DER SPEED OF LIGHT, VOT IS 300,000 KM/SEC.
IF IT VAS ONLY A FEW METERS A SECOND, LIFE AS VE KNOW IT VOULD BE ABSOLUTELY IMPOSSIBLE - HUR-HUR-HUR!

IF AN ASTRONAUT WERE TO STAY IN ORBIT FOR SIX MONTHS, THAT IS, OVER FIFTEEN MILLION SECONDS...

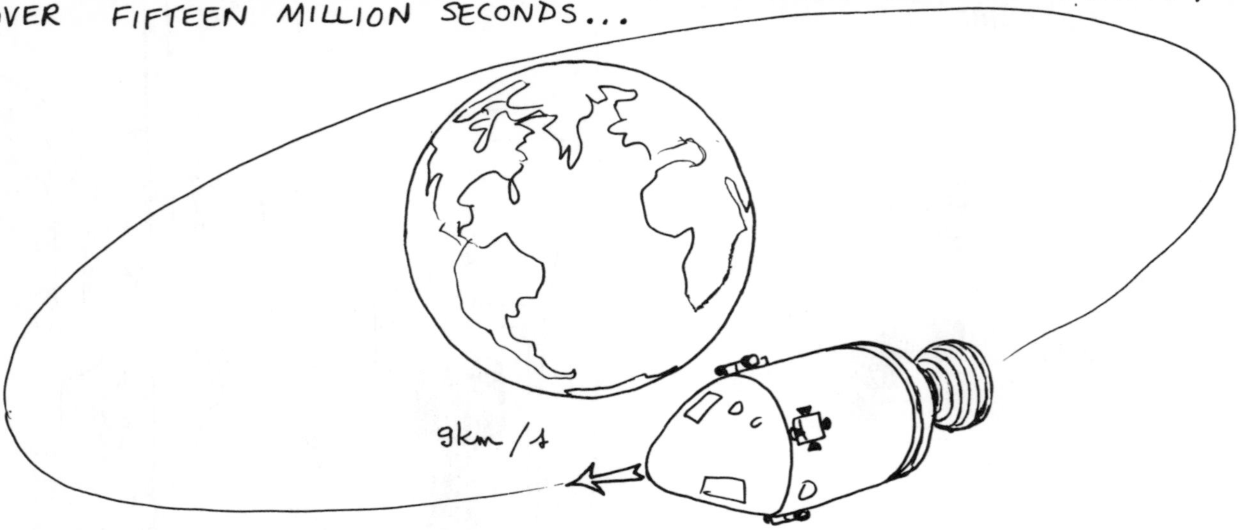

... THEN HIS AGE WOULD BE RETARDED BY 1.4 HUNDREDTHS OF A SECOND.

AT THE MOMENT IT'S ONLY OF INTEREST TO SPECIALISTS IN HIGH ENERGY PHYSICS(*)...

... AND CERTAIN GOVERNMENT AGENCIES...

(*) ALSO CALLED PLUTOPHYSICS BECAUSE IT'S NOT EXACTLY CHEAP...

WHEN I GO FASTER, DOES IT REALLY CAUSE THE UNIVERSE TO SHRINK?
SOMETHIN' ROUND HERE NEEDS A SHRINK, I CAN TELL YA.
ENTERPRISE TO MISSION CONTROL: WE HAVE LIFT-OFF.
THAT'S REALLY A SPACED-OUT CORVETTE...
TEN THOUSAND KILOMETERS PER SECOND. ALL SYSTEMS NORMAL. I'LL ACCELERATE!

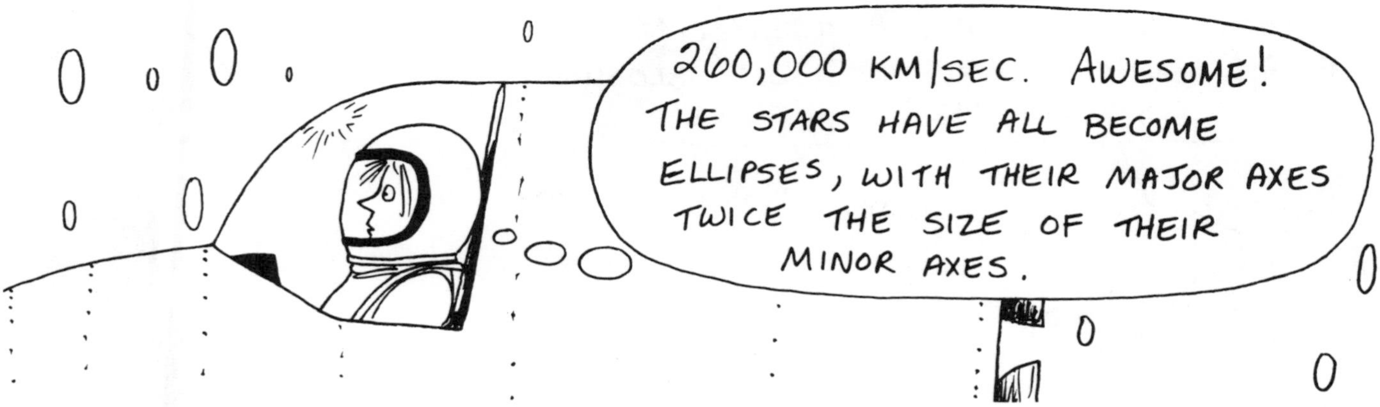
260,000 KM/SEC. AWESOME! THE STARS HAVE ALL BECOME ELLIPSES, WITH THEIR MAJOR AXES TWICE THE SIZE OF THEIR MINOR AXES.

MEMORANDUM

IN FACT ARCHIBALD HIGGINS COULD NOT REALLY OBSERVE THIS **LORENTZ CONTRACTION**, FOR THE EXCELLENT REASON THAT **EVERYTHING** CONTRACTS: THE UNIVERSE, ARCHIBALD, AND HIS SHUTTLE.

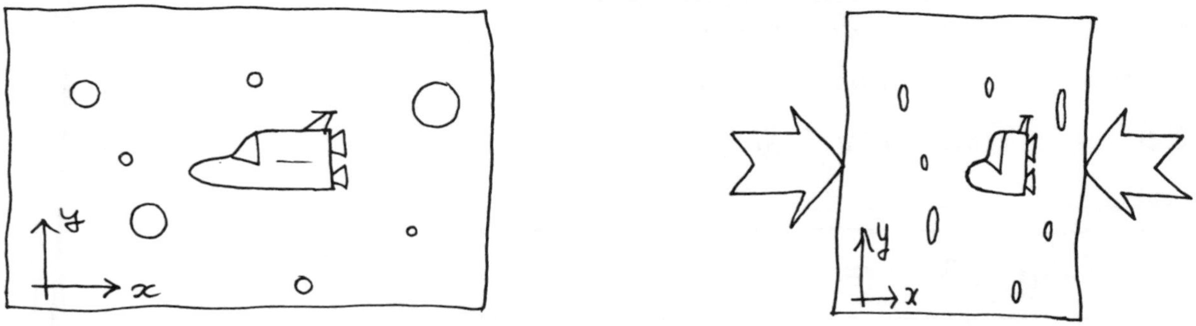
y
x
y
x

IN THE SAME WAY, TRAVELERS IN COSMIC PARK DON'T NOTICE ANY SHRINKAGE.

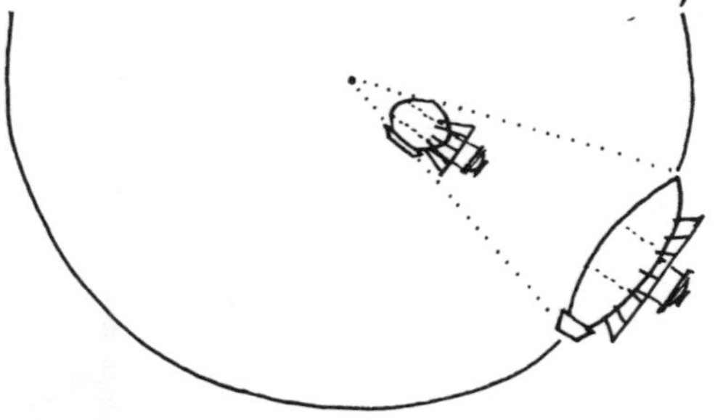

The Boss

SO IF I SPEED UP A BIT – LITTLE OLD ME, TIRESIAS THE SNAIL – I SQUASH UP THE ENTIRE UNIVERSE LIKE AN ACCORDION IN THE DIRECTION I'M MOVING.
WHAT POWER!

THAT'S REE-DICKLUS! A TIDDLY LITTLE SNAIL CAN'T SHRINK THE 'OLE BLOOMIN' YOUNYVERSE!
EEEP!
IT'S NOT A MATTER OF SHRINKING THE UNIVERSE, OR SLOWING THE PASSAGE OF TIME. DISTANCES AND TIMES ARE ONLY APPEARANCES. EVERYTHING IS AN ILLUSION AND NOTHING IS ABSOLUTE. THAT'S THE WORLD OF RELATIVITY.
SO WHAT IS THE UNIVERSE LIKE?
IT DEPENDS ON THE SPEED OF THE OBSERVER.
SPEED RELATIVE TO WHAT?
THE ESSENTIAL IDEA IS THAT TWO PEOPLE GOING AT THE SAME SPEED V IN THE SAME DIRECTION SHOULD SEE - AND EXPERIENCE - THE UNIVERSE IN THE SAME WAY.
BUT BACK TO COSMIC PARK. YOU'LL SEE THAT FOR SOME BEINGS, THE UNIVERSE HAS A SINGULAR ALLURE...

WHEN TIME STANDS STILL

OR: LIFE AMONG THE PHOTONS

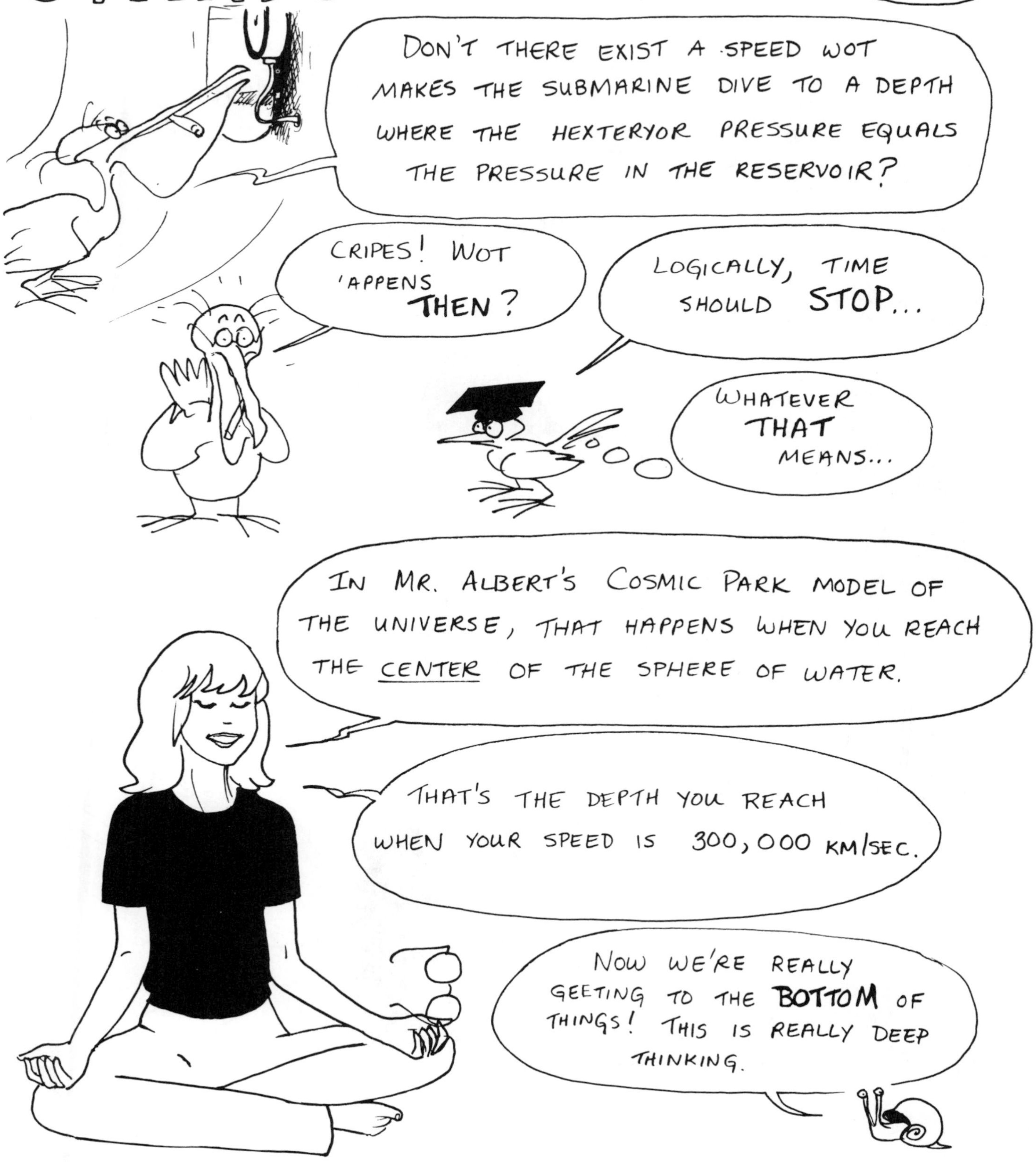
DON'T THERE EXIST A SPEED WOT MAKES THE SUBMARINE DIVE TO A DEPTH WHERE THE HEXTERYOR PRESSURE EQUALS THE PRESSURE IN THE RESERVOIR?
CRIPES! WOT 'APPENS THEN?
LOGICALLY, TIME SHOULD STOP...
WHATEVER THAT MEANS...
IN MR. ALBERT'S COSMIC PARK MODEL OF THE UNIVERSE, THAT HAPPENS WHEN YOU REACH THE CENTER OF THE SPHERE OF WATER.
THAT'S THE DEPTH YOU REACH WHEN YOUR SPEED IS 300,000 KM/SEC.
NOW WE'RE REALLY GEETING TO THE BOTTOM OF THINGS! THIS IS REALLY DEEP THINKING.

DOES ANYTHING EXIST AT THE BOTTOM OF ALL THIS CHRONOS, AT THE CENTER OF THINGS, WHERE REIGNS THE ABSOLUTE ZERO OF TIME?
TIME— THAT'S FOR OTHER FOLKS TO WORRY ABOUT.
WE DON'T BOTHER WITH THAT STUFF!
YES— PHOTONS.
THE CONSTITUENT PARTICLES OF LIGHT.
EVEN SO, I CAN STILL MEASURE HOW FAST PHOTONS TRAVEL. THEY MOVE THROUGH A DISTANCE D IN A TIME t, AND THEIR SPEED IS D/t = 300,000 KM/SEC. I HAVE A FUNNY FEELING I'VE SEEN THAT NUMBER BEFORE...
THEY'RE BORN— THEN THEY DIE— IN A FLASH!
BLEB BLEB
YES— THAT REALLY IS LIFE IN THE FAST LANE...

EXISTING IN TIME, THAT'S JUST YOUR WAY OF LIFE. PHOTONS HAVE A DIFFERENT LIFESTYLE. FOR THEM BIRTH AND DEATH ARE TWO CONSECUTIVE EVENTS.
DOES THAT MEAN THAT FOR PHOTONS, THERE'S NO SENSE TO TIME?
THE PROPER TIME OF THE PHOTON TAKES PLACE IN AN INFINITELY THIN PRESENT, SANDWICHED BETWEEN THE INSTANT OF ITS BIRTH AND THE INSTANT OF ITS DEATH. CONSIDER A THREE-DIMENSIONAL SPACE-TIME WITH COORDINATES (x,y,t). IF YOU FLATTEN IT IN THE TIME DIRECTION YOU'RE LEFT WITH A SURFACE THAT STILL HAS TWO SIDES. THE DISTINCTION BETWEEN THESE TWO SIDES DEFINES THE DIRECTION OF TIME FOR THE PHOTON.
OH, WOE!
DEATH
t
y
x
BIRTH
DEATH
BIRTH

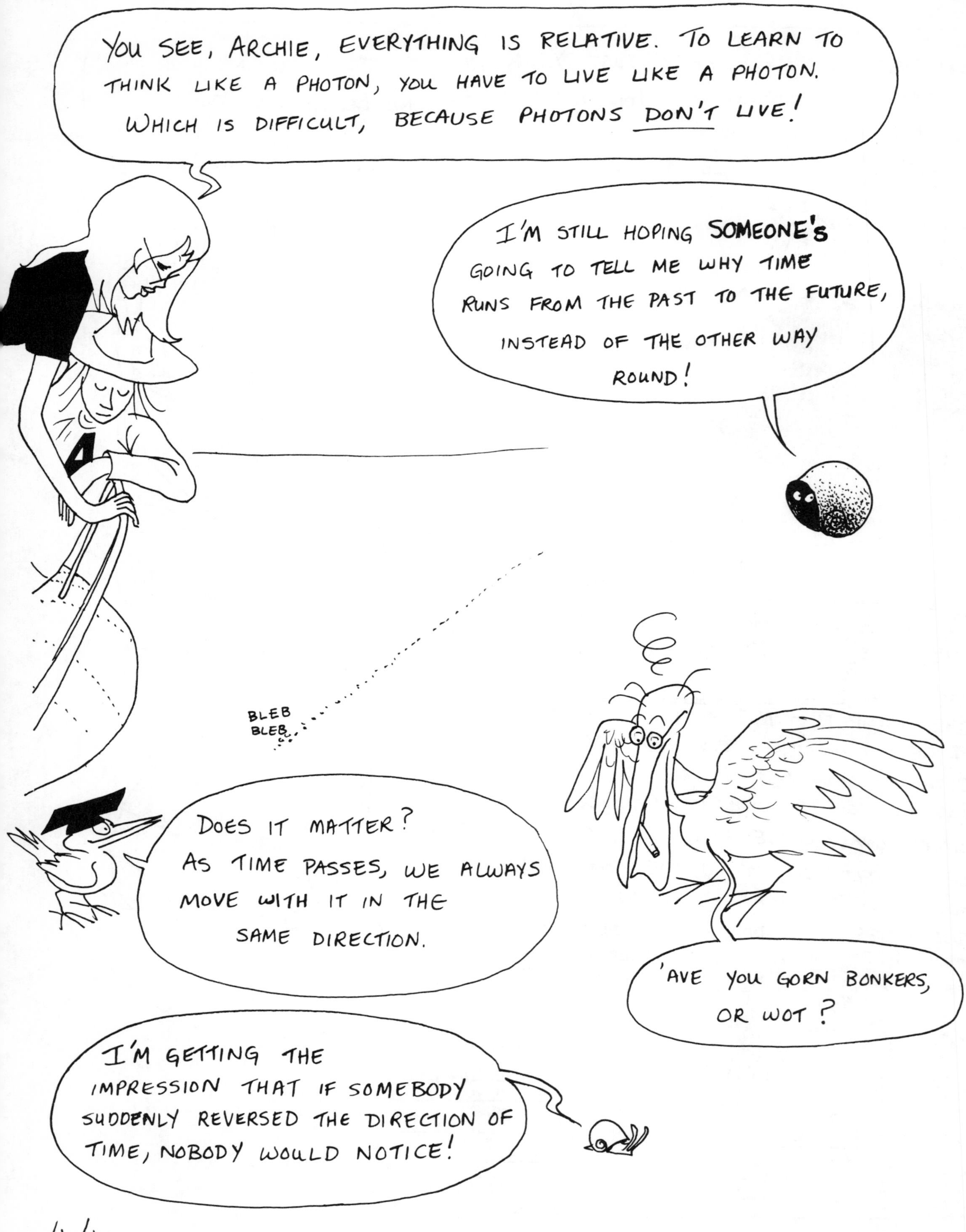
YOU SEE, ARCHIE, EVERYTHING IS RELATIVE. TO LEARN TO THINK LIKE A PHOTON, YOU HAVE TO LIVE LIKE A PHOTON. WHICH IS DIFFICULT, BECAUSE PHOTONS DON'T LIVE!
I'M STILL HOPING SOMEONE'S GOING TO TELL ME WHY TIME RUNS FROM THE PAST TO THE FUTURE, INSTEAD OF THE OTHER WAY ROUND!
BLEB BLEB
DOES IT MATTER? AS TIME PASSES, WE ALWAYS MOVE WITH IT IN THE SAME DIRECTION.
'AVE YOU GORN BONKERS, OR WOT?
I'M GETTING THE IMPRESSION THAT IF SOMEBODY SUDDENLY REVERSED THE DIRECTION OF TIME, NOBODY WOULD NOTICE!

YOU KNOW, I THINK I'D QUITE ENJOY BEING A PHOTON – EVEN IF ONLY FOR AN INSTANT– TO GET AN IDEA OF HOW THEY VIEW THE UNIVERSE.
IT'S NOT POSSIBLE TO DRAW A 4-DIMENSIONAL SPACE-TIME. BUT YOU CAN, IN THREE DIMENSIONS, SKETCH THE INTERTWINED TRAJECTORIES FOLLOWED BY ALL OF THE OBJECTS IN THE UNIVERSE (THAT IS, ALL PARTICLES) AS THEY WOULD BE SEEN BY A HYPOTHETICAL OBSERVER WHO IS AT REST.
A SORT O' PIN-UP PHOTO IN THREE DIMENSIONS...
A
A REAL CAN OF WORMS!
YOU GET SOMETHING LIKE A PLATE OF SPAGHETTI, OR THE LOS ANGELES FREEWAY SYSTEM...

AS FAR AS **LENGTHS** GO, THIS UNIVERSE IS ELASTIC. IF ANOTHER OBSERVER MOVES AT A VELOCITY $\vec{V}$ IN SOME DIRECTION, THEN EVERYTHING HAPPENS AS IF THE UNIVERSE (AND THE OBSERVER) HAS SHRUNK IN THIS DIRECTION.

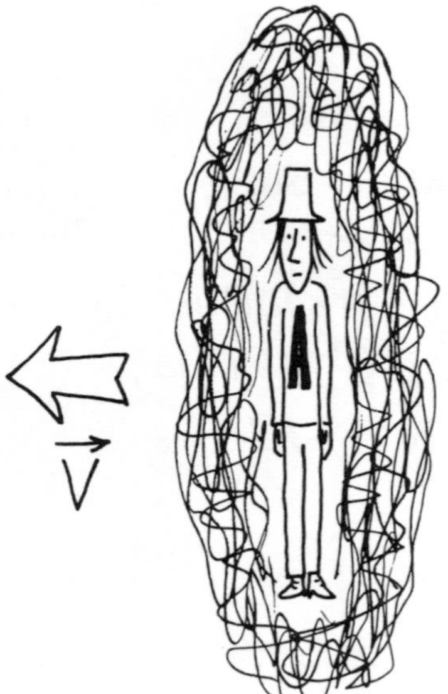
$\vec{V}$

$\vec{V}$

THE PHOTON TAKES THIS CONTRACTION EFFECT TO EXTREMES. WE'VE ALREADY SEEN HOW ITS **PROPER TIME** IS SQUASHED COMPLETELY FLAT. IF IT COULD PERCEIVE THE UNIVERSE, IT WOULD APPEAR TO BE FLATTENED LIKE A PANCAKE ALONG THE DIRECTION OF **MOTION**. SO THE PHOTON INHABITS A <u>TWO</u>-DIMENSIONAL WORLD... AND THE PHOTON ITSELF IS SITUATED WITHIN THAT WORLD LIKE A SMALL, FLAT SCRIBBLE.

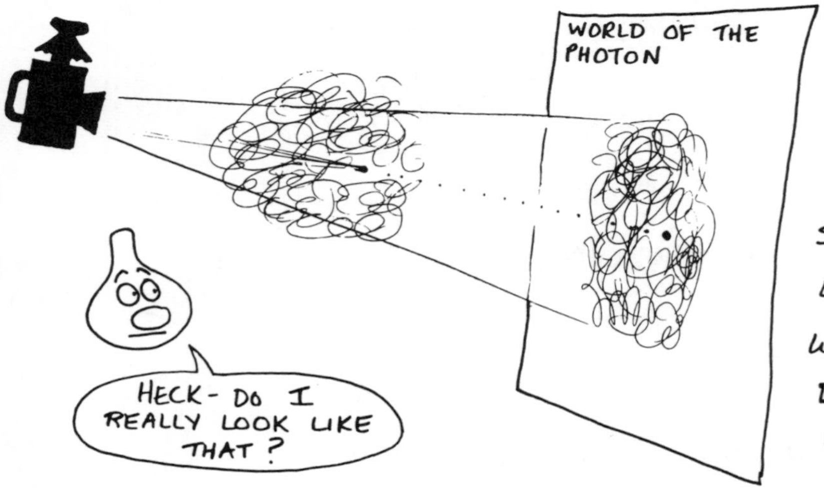
WORLD OF THE PHOTON
HECK- DO I REALLY LOOK LIKE THAT?

IT'S RATHER LIKE THE EFFECT YOU'D GET BY PROJECTING ON TO A SCREEN A PICTURE OF A BALL OF SPAGHETTI (AS SEEN BY A MOTIONLESS OBSERVER) USING A LAMP WHOSE AXIS IS ALIGNED WITH THE DIRECTION IN WHICH THE PHOTON IS MOVING.

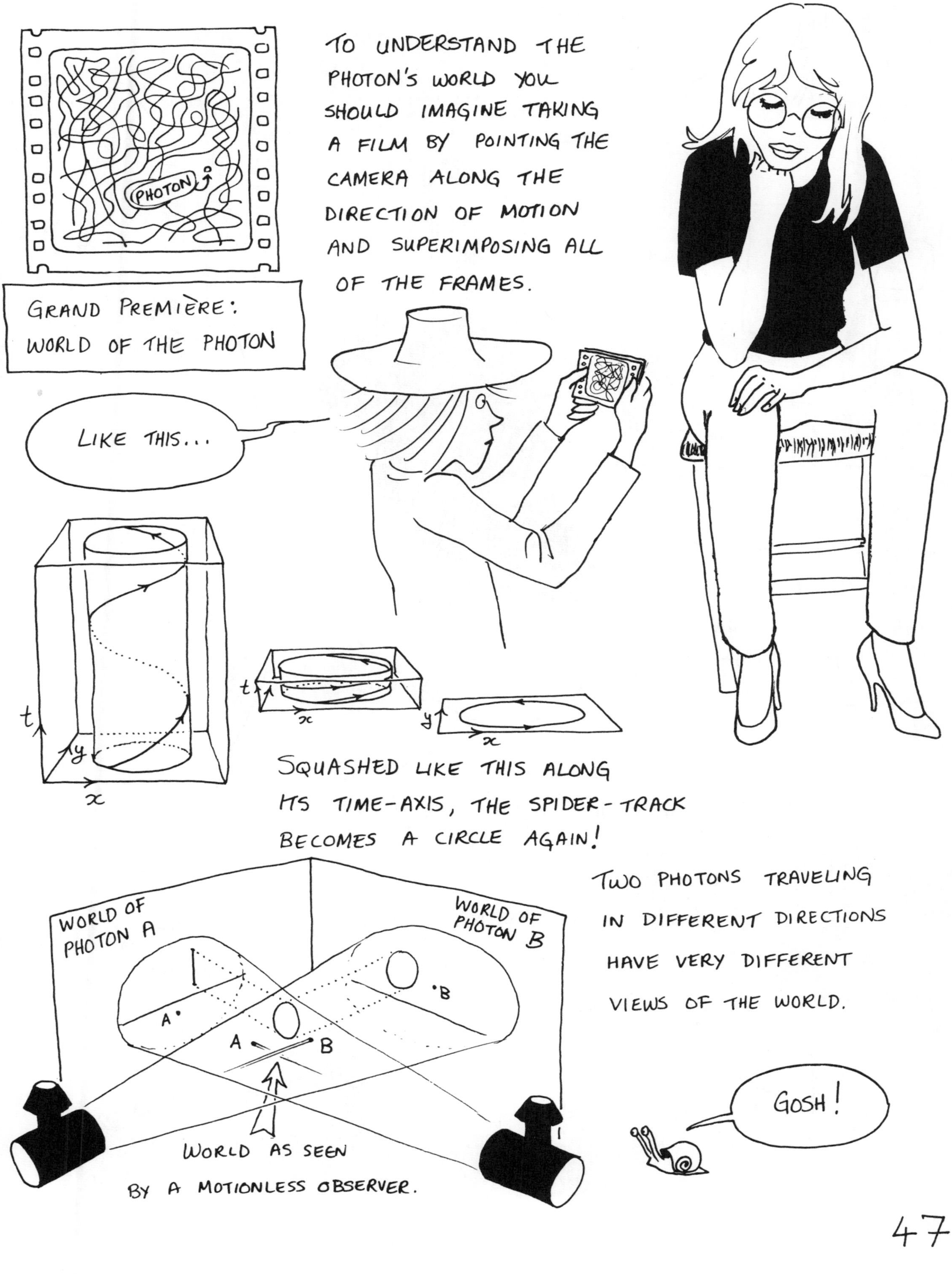
PHOTON
TO UNDERSTAND THE PHOTON'S WORLD YOU SHOULD IMAGINE TAKING A FILM BY POINTING THE CAMERA ALONG THE DIRECTION OF MOTION AND SUPERIMPOSING ALL OF THE FRAMES.
GRAND PREMIÈRE: WORLD OF THE PHOTON
LIKE THIS...
t
y
x
SQUASHED LIKE THIS ALONG ITS TIME-AXIS, THE SPIDER-TRACK BECOMES A CIRCLE AGAIN!
WORLD OF PHOTON A
WORLD OF PHOTON B
A
B
A
B
WORLD AS SEEN BY A MOTIONLESS OBSERVER.
TWO PHOTONS TRAVELING IN DIFFERENT DIRECTIONS HAVE VERY DIFFERENT VIEWS OF THE WORLD.
GOSH!

YES, BUT WHAT IS THE UNIVERSE?
EVERYTHING AND NOTHING AT THE SAME TIME. THERE ARE A THOUSAND AND ONE WAYS TO SEE IT, OR LIVE IT.
x's, y's, t's — IT'S ALL HOGWASH, THAT'S WHAT IT IS!
NO IT'S NOT— IT'S ALGEBRA.
DESPITE WHICH, IT HAS ITS USES!
t
y
x

INVARIANCE OF THE SPEED OF LIGHT
VARIATION OF MASS

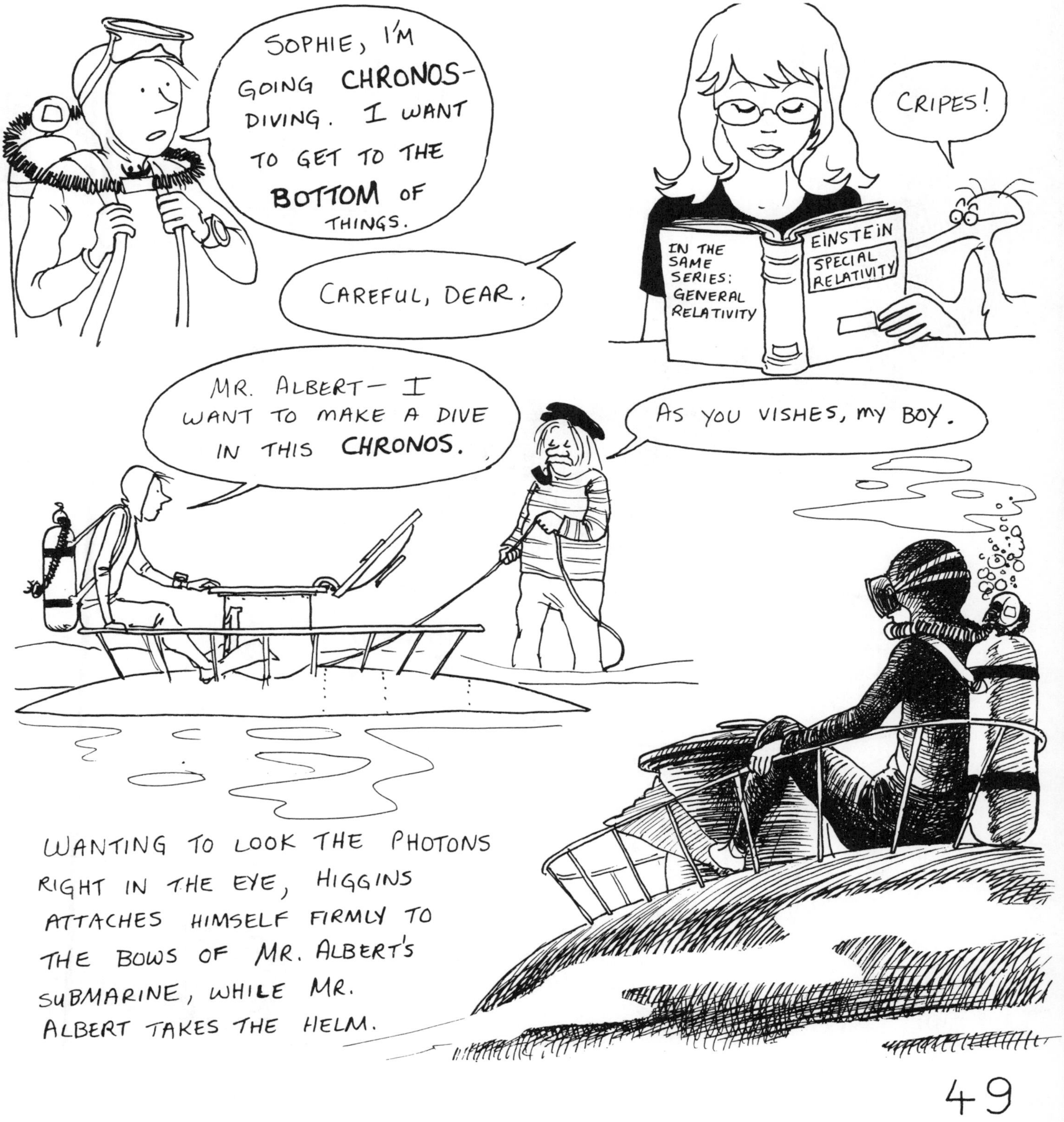

SOPHIE, I'M GOING CHRONOS-DIVING. I WANT TO GET TO THE BOTTOM OF THINGS.
CAREFUL, DEAR.
EINSTEIN
SPECIAL RELATIVITY
IN THE SAME SERIES: GENERAL RELATIVITY
CRIPES!
MR. ALBERT— I WANT TO MAKE A DIVE IN THIS CHRONOS.
AS YOU VISHES, MY BOY.
WANTING TO LOOK THE PHOTONS RIGHT IN THE EYE, HIGGINS ATTACHES HIMSELF FIRMLY TO THE BOWS OF MR. ALBERT'S SUBMARINE, WHILE MR. ALBERT TAKES THE HELM.

PHOTONS! I CAN SEE THEM!
THIS CHRONOS ISN'T HALF **DEEP**!
MY DEPTHMETER INDICATES A SPEED V_1.
THAT PHOTON'S GONE A **DISTANCE** D_1 IN TIME t_1.
I DIVIDE D_1 BY t_1 AND GET 300,000 KM/SEC.
FASTER, MR. ALBERT, AND DON'T SPARE THE SEAHORSES!

ALL OBSERVERS, WHATEVER THEIR VELOCITY, GET THE IDENTICAL VALUE c WHEN THEY MEASURE THE SPEED OF PHOTONS – THE FUNDAMENTAL PARTICLES OF LIGHT. THEY OCCUPY A SPECIAL PLACE IN COSMIC PARK. EVERYTHING HAPPENS AS IF THEY BEHAVED LIKE SMALL SEARCHLIGHTS WHOSE 'RAYS' MOVE AT A CONSTANT ANGULAR VELOCITY, PROJECTING THEIR IMAGES ON ALL OF THE CONCENTRIC SPHERES THAT GO TO MAKE UP **CHRONOS**. BECAUSE OF COMPENSATING CHANGES IN DISTANCES AND PROPER TIMES, OBSERVERS INVARIABLY FIND THAT $c = D/t$ = 300,000 KM/SEC.

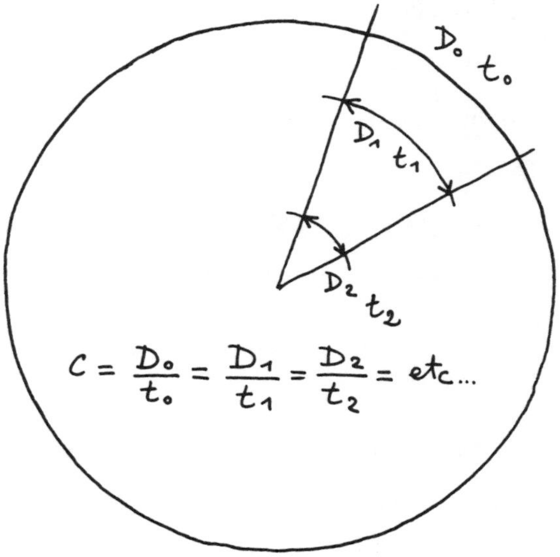

THIS ABSOLUTE CONSTANCY OF THE SPEED OF LIGHT (THAT IS, THE SPEED OF PHOTONS) WAS FIRST OBSERVED EXPERIMENTALLY BY MICHELSON AND MORLEY IN 1881. THIRTY-FOUR YEARS LATER, IN 1915, EINSTEIN THREW THE TRADITIONAL MODEL OF SPACE-TIME OUT THE WINDOW, BECAUSE IT WAS INCOMPATIBLE WITH THIS INVARIANCE. HE SET ABOUT FINDING A NEW SPACE-TIME, THAT OF RELATIVITY. COSMIC PARK GIVES US SOME IDEA OF WHAT THIS IS LIKE.

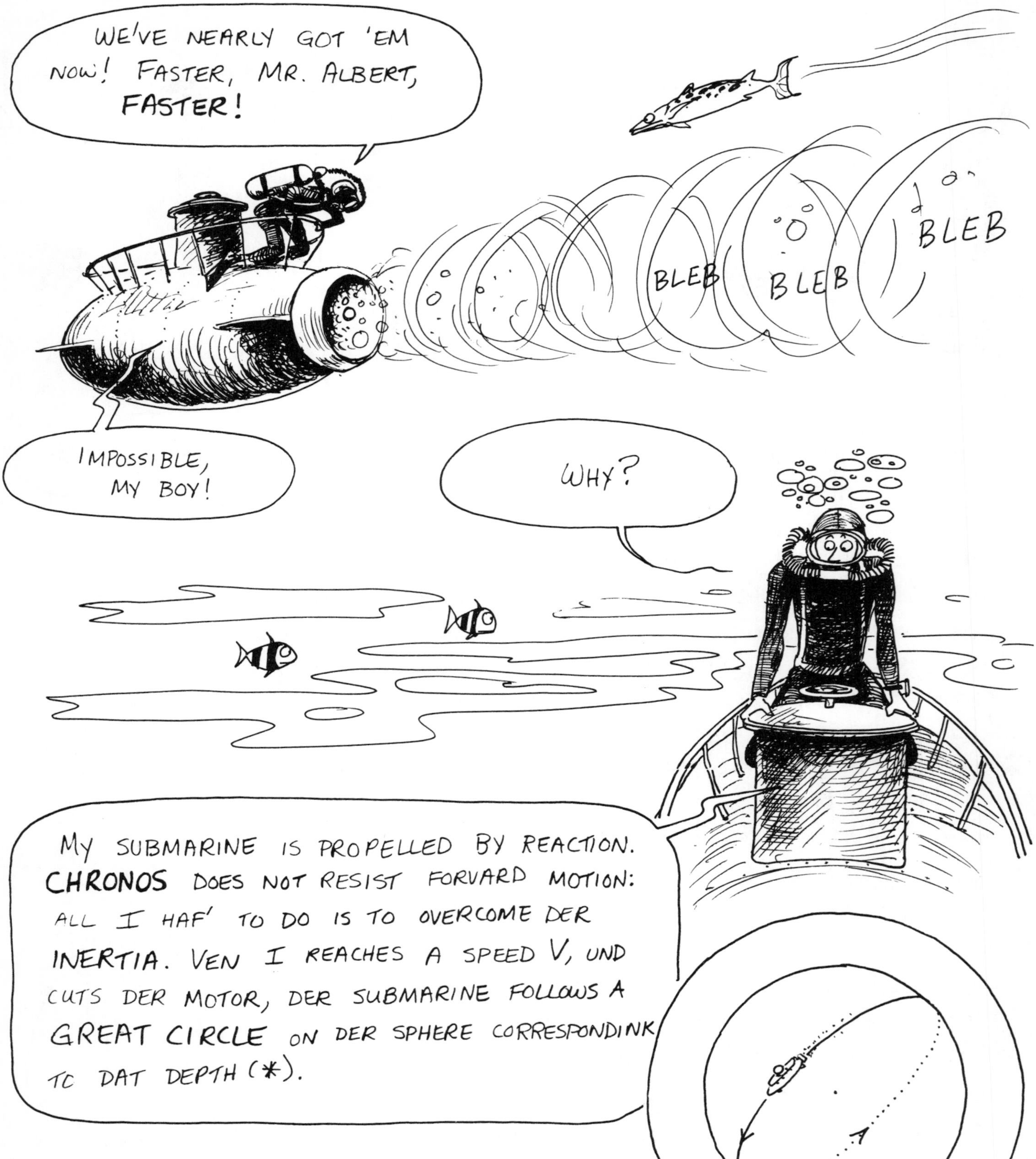

(*) IN OTHER WORDS, A GEODESIC ON THE SPHERE. SEE <u>HERE'S LOOKING AT EUCLID</u>, SAME SERIES.

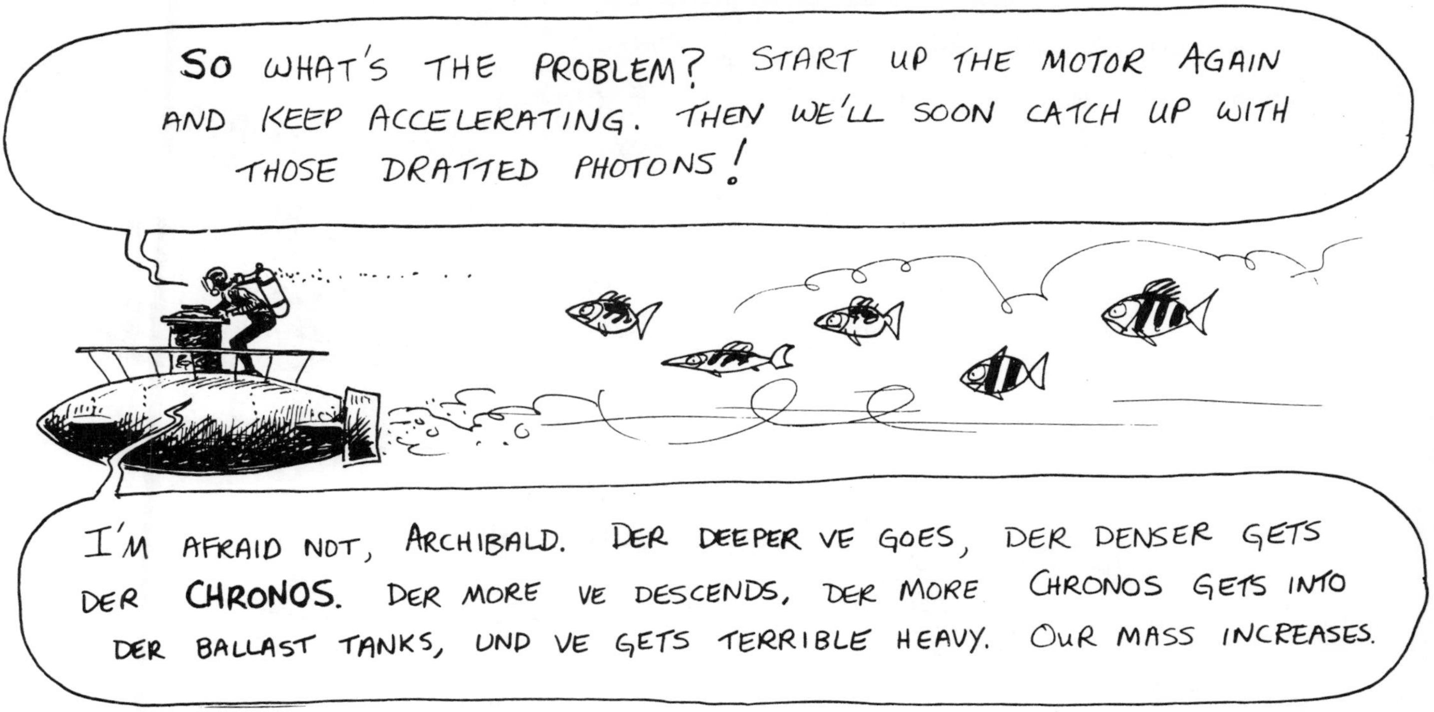
SO WHAT'S THE PROBLEM? START UP THE MOTOR AGAIN AND KEEP ACCELERATING. THEN WE'LL SOON CATCH UP WITH THOSE DRATTED PHOTONS!
I'M AFRAID NOT, ARCHIBALD. DER DEEPER VE GOES, DER DENSER GETS DER CHRONOS. DER MORE VE DESCENDS, DER MORE CHRONOS GETS INTO DER BALLAST TANKS, UND VE GETS TERRIBLE HEAVY. OUR MASS INCREASES.

MEMORANDUM:

WE WISH TO DISPEL A COMMON MISCONCEPTION — THAT EXERCISE MAKES YOU LOSE WEIGHT. ACTUALLY, THE OPPOSITE IS TRUE! THE SIMPLE ACT OF LEAVING A REST STATE (MASS m_0) INCREASES THE MASS m ACCORDING TO THE RELATION $m = \frac{m_0}{\sqrt{1 - \frac{v^2}{c^2}}}$. OF COURSE, WHEN YOU STOP, YOU RETURN TO YOUR ORIGINAL MASS m_0.

The Boss

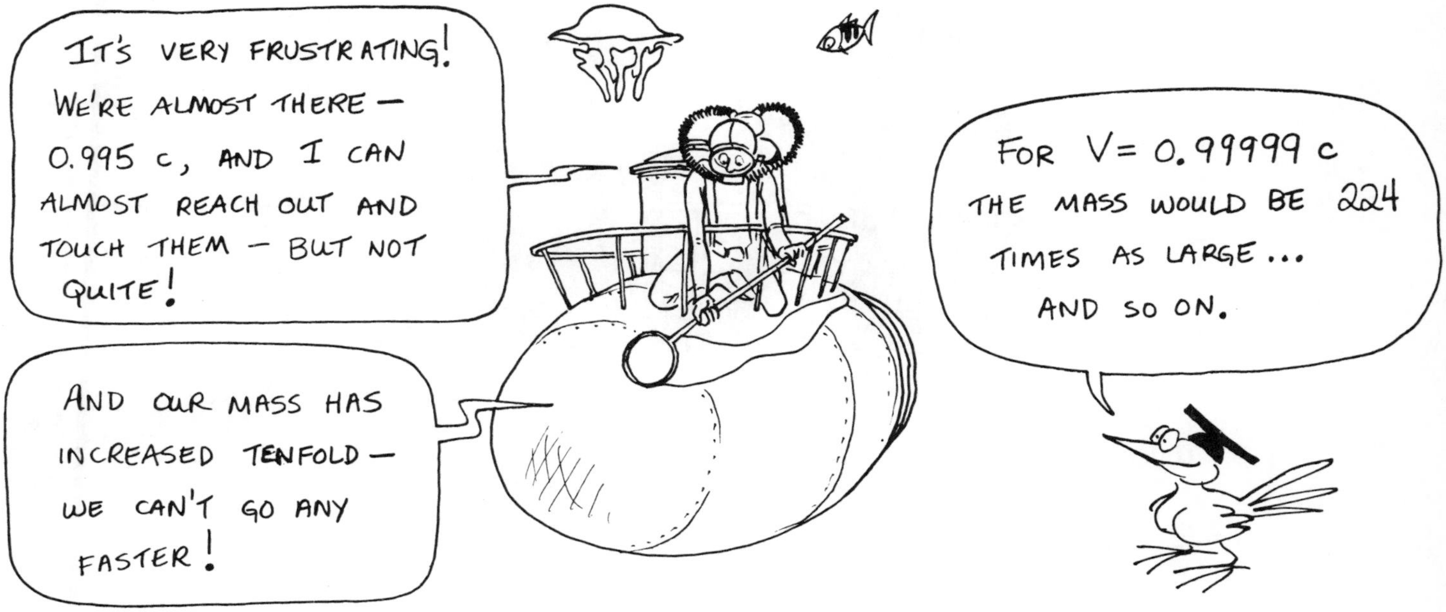
IT'S VERY FRUSTRATING! WE'RE ALMOST THERE — 0.995 c, AND I CAN ALMOST REACH OUT AND TOUCH THEM — BUT NOT QUITE!
AND OUR MASS HAS INCREASED TENFOLD — WE CAN'T GO ANY FASTER!
FOR V= 0.99999 c THE MASS WOULD BE 224 TIMES AS LARGE... AND SO ON.

GOINK ON VOULD SURF NO USEFUL PORPOISE... VE IS CONSUMINK AN INFINITE AMOUNT OF ENERGY IF VE CHASES DER PHOTONS. GET READY, I'M SURFACING!
OH, SHUCKS!
WROAR!
PHEEEEW! YOU WON'T GET THAT AT DISNEYWORLD!
IF I UNDERSTAND YOU, THE MORE ENERGY YOU GIVE TO A BODY, THE GREATER ITS MASS BECOMES.
JA. DAT MAKES SENSE, BECAUSE DER MASS UND DER ENERGY ARE DER SAME T'ING.
E = m

VELL— UP TO A CONSTANT FACTOR... VICH IS DER SQUARE OF c. SO VE CAN WRITE $E=mc^2$. HMMM... IT'S A SIMPLE MATTER OF UNITS. IF OUR UNIT OF LENGTH VAS 300,000 KM DEN VE'D HAVE YUST:
$E=m$
WHERE DOES THIS VALUE FOR c OF 300,000 KM/SEC COME FROM?
IF I VAS YOU, I'D PUT IT DER UDDER WAY ROUN'. VERE DOES DESE KILOMETERS AND SECONDS COME FROM?
I— ER— WHAT?
c IS THE UNIT OF SPEED PAR EXCELLENCE. THE UNIVERSAL COSMIC STANDARD. THE KILOMETER PER SECOND IS JUST A MISERABLE SUBMULTIPLE.

(*) FROM EPISTEMOLOGY (THEORY OF KNOWLEDGE) AND COP: THOUGHT POLICE.

THE EDIFICE OF SCIENCE IS SUBJECT TO PARADIGM-SHOCK. OVER AND OVER AGAIN IT CRACKS, COLLAPSES, AND IS REBORN FROM ITS OWN RUINS.

NOW, I WONDER WHAT HE MEANT BY THAT?
A
JUST THAT, IN SPACE-TIME, THE STRAIGHT LINE (1) FROM A TO B IS THE LONGEST PATH BETWEEN THEM.

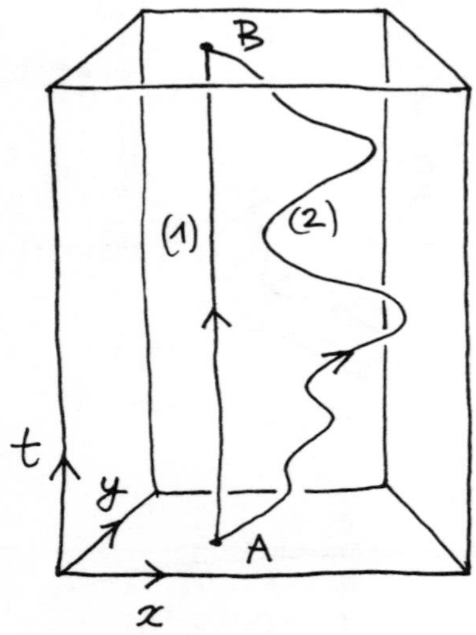
B
(1)
(2)
t
y
A
x

FOR INSTANCE, THE STRAIGHT SEGMENT $\overline{AB}$ IS THE PATH YOU'D FOLLOW IF YOU WERE MOTIONLESS. THE CURVED PATH (2) BRINGS EFFECTS OF <u>VELOCITY</u> INTO PLAY. WE'VE ALREADY SEEN THAT WHEN YOU MOVE, YOUR <u>PROPER TIME</u> (THAT OF THE TRAVELER, NOT OF A STATIONARY OBSERVER) FLOWS MORE SLOWLY.

THE TRUE MEASURE OF DISTANCE, IN SPACE-TIME, IS HOW MUCH PROPER TIME HAS PASSED. SO FROM THIS VIEWPOINT, THE CURVED PATH BECOMES <u>SHORTER</u> THAN THE STRAIGHT ONE.

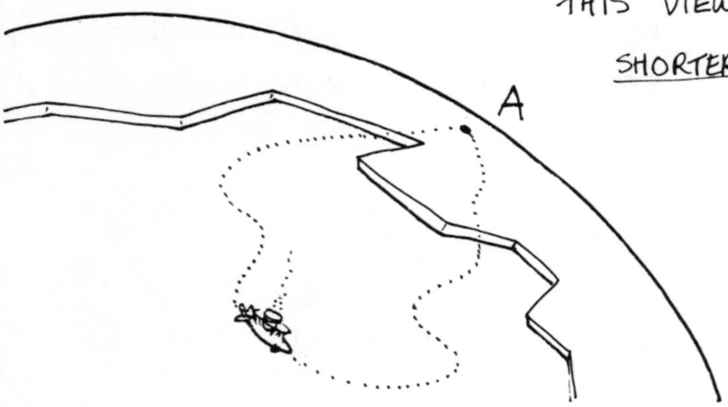
A

It's STUPID, having to follow a path ter stay in the same place!

THE IMPOSSIBLE JOURNEY

Night falls in Cosmic Park
Sophie – what are stars?
Suns like our own.
Our star has its own planet: the Earth. Do you think that other stars might also have their own planets?
Sure, Archie.

HOW FAR AWAY IS THE NEAREST STAR?
LIGHT TAKES FOUR YEARS TO REACH US FROM OUR NEAREST NEIGHBOR, PROXIMA CENTAURI.
THAT'S... 40 TRILLION KILOMETERS!
WHEREAS PLUTO, OUT ON THE EDGE OF THE SOLAR SYSTEM, IS ABOUT 5 BILLION KILOMETERS – THAT IS, 5 LIGHT-HOURS.
SO PROXIMA CENTAURI IS TEN THOUSAND TIMES FURTHER AWAY... GOSH, THE UNIVERSE IS A BIG PLACE!

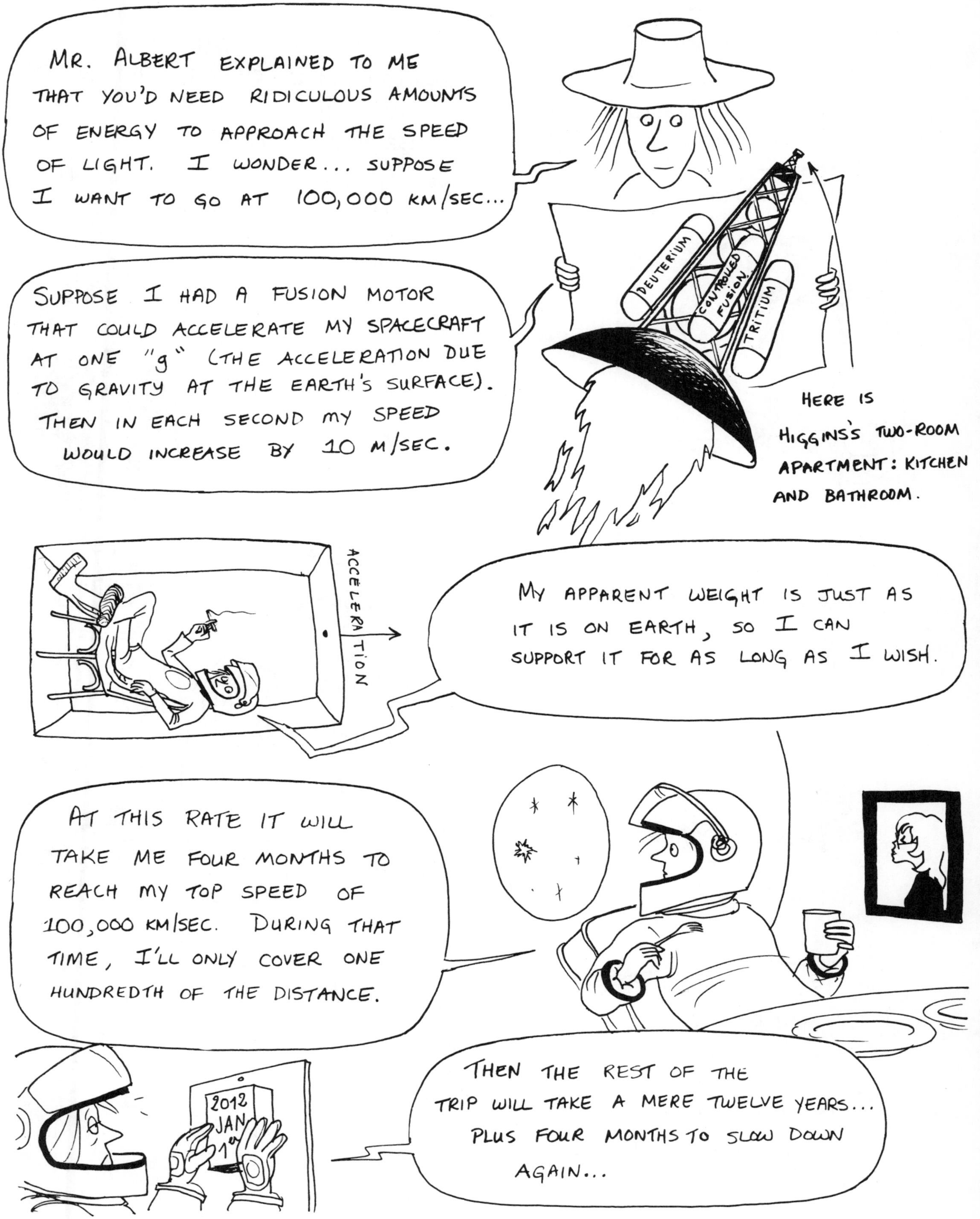
MR. ALBERT EXPLAINED TO ME THAT YOU'D NEED RIDICULOUS AMOUNTS OF ENERGY TO APPROACH THE SPEED OF LIGHT. I WONDER... SUPPOSE I WANT TO GO AT 100,000 KM/SEC...
DEUTERIUM
CONTROLLED FUSION
TRITIUM
SUPPOSE I HAD A FUSION MOTOR THAT COULD ACCELERATE MY SPACECRAFT AT ONE "g" (THE ACCELERATION DUE TO GRAVITY AT THE EARTH'S SURFACE). THEN IN EACH SECOND MY SPEED WOULD INCREASE BY 10 M/SEC.
HERE IS HIGGINS'S TWO-ROOM APARTMENT: KITCHEN AND BATHROOM.
ACCELERATION
MY APPARENT WEIGHT IS JUST AS IT IS ON EARTH, SO I CAN SUPPORT IT FOR AS LONG AS I WISH.
AT THIS RATE IT WILL TAKE ME FOUR MONTHS TO REACH MY TOP SPEED OF 100,000 KM/SEC. DURING THAT TIME, I'LL ONLY COVER ONE HUNDREDTH OF THE DISTANCE.
2012 JAN
THEN THE REST OF THE TRIP WILL TAKE A MERE TWELVE YEARS... PLUS FOUR MONTHS TO SLOW DOWN AGAIN...

AND THE SAME AGAIN IF I WANT TO COME BACK TO TELL PEOPLE WHAT I FOUND THERE...
YES... AND ALTHOUGH THERE'S PRECIOUS LITTLE CHANCE THAT WE'RE THE ONLY LIVING CREATURES IN THE UNIVERSE, THE NEAREST INHABITED PLANET (IF THERE IS ONE) WILL PROBABLY BE A LOT FURTHER AWAY THAN FOUR LIGHT-YEARS!
YOU'RE TELLING ME THAT STAR-TRAVEL ACCORDING TO THE LAWS OF COSMIC PARK IS A LIFETIME CAREER.
SO... WHAT TO DO?
IS THE VOYAGE FOREVER IMPOSSIBLE?
DOES THE LAD NEVER GIVE UP?

TO GO FASTER THAN THE SPEED OF LIGHT MAKES NO SENSE. IT'S LIKE TRYING TO DIVE DEEPER THAN THE CENTER OF COSMIC PARK!
OF COURSE, COSMIC PARK MAY NOT BE THE ULTIMATE MODEL.
VERY LIKELY. BUT THAT DOESN'T TELL ME HOW TO REACH THE STARS IN A REASONABLE TIME.

PERHAPS IT'LL ALWAYS BE IMPOSSIBLE?
HMMMMMM...
HOW ABOUT...

I KNOW HOW YOU COULD DO IT...
TIRESIAS!

THE END

MAX – DO YOU THINK ONE DAY PEOPLE WILL GO TO THE STARS?